MURDER AT ELSTREE

or

Mr. Thurtell and His Gig

By THOMAS BURKE

British Library Cataloguing-in-Publication Data
A catalogue record for this book is available from the
British Library

Thomas Burke

Thomas Burke was born in Clapham, London in 1886. His father died when he was very young, and at the age of ten he was removed to a home for middle-class boys who were "respectably descended but without adequate means to their support." Burke published his first piece of writing – a short story entitled 'The Bellamy Diamonds' – in 1901, when he was just fifteen. However, proper recognition came in 1916, with the publication of *Limehouse Nights,* a collection of melodramatic short stories set amongst the immigrant population of London's Chinatown. *Limehouse Nights* was serialized in three British periodicals, *The English Review, Colour* and *The New Witness,* and received positive attention from reviewers and a number of authors, including H. G. Wells. It also sparked something of a controversy, however, and was initially banned by libraries due to the scandalous interracial relationships it portrayed between Chinese men and white women.

It was these portrayals of London's Chinatown that Burke is best-remembered for. However, there is some degree of confusion over how much of Burke's writing was based in fact; as literary critic Anne Witchard states, most of what we know about Burke's life is based on works that "purport to be autobiographical, yet contain far more invention than truth." Whatever the truth, there is no doubt that, in his day, Burke was regarded as the foremost chronicler of London's Chinatown at the turn-of-the-century. Burke told newspaper journalists that he had "sat at the feet of Chinese philosophers who kept opium dens to learn from the lips that could frame only broken English, the secrets, good and evil, of the mysterious East," and these journalists almost uniformly took him at his word.

Burke continued to use descriptions of urban London life as a focus of his writing throughout his life. Off the back of *Limehouse Nights,* Burke published the thematically similar *Twinkletoes* in 1918, and *More Limehouse Nights* in 1921. However, he was a prolific author who tried his hand at a number of different genres. He semi-regularly published essays on the London environment, including pieces such as 'The Real East End' and 'London in My Times', and during the thirties even tried his hand at horror fiction. Indeed, in 1949, shortly after his death, Burke's short story 'The Hands of Ottermole' was voted the best mystery of all time by critics. Burke also influenced the burgeoning film industry in Hollywood; D W Griffith, for example, used the short story 'The Chink and the Child' from *Limehouse Nights* (1917) as basis for his silent movie, *Broken Blossoms* (1919), and Charlie Chaplin derived 'A Dog's Life' (1918) from the same book.

By THOMAS BURKE

NOTE

Some readers may think that a passage at the end of Chapter I bears a resemblance to a passage in Borrow's *Lavengro*. It does. It is that passage.

The rest of the story, of course, is based on the historic Elstree Murder of 1823.

CONTENTS

MURDER AT ELSTREE

I

On that May morning of 1821 the roads around
the grey city of Norwich were streaming and
twinkling with traffic. Coaches, chaises, gigs,
barouches, dennets, tilburies and phaetons jogged
and glided. Their occupants, both elegant and
coarse, bawled to each other, offering or taking
odds. Alongside them tramped the citizens and
villagers and other humble supporters of 'the
fancy.' The vehicles knew where they were
going. They were going to the secret rendezvous where the great knuckle turn-up was to
come off. The walkers, who had not learned the
secret, had only to follow them.

By following them along the white road, and

B   I bathing in the dust thrown up by hoofs and wheels, the walkers came at length to what usually was a secluded corner of Mousehold Heath, but was to-day more popular and populous than the main streets of the city.

Under the high noon sun, specimens of all ranks, from castle to slum, were gathered and, for the moment, were equal. Dusty and stained, they paraded the heathery turf and gazed at the notables while they waited for the arrival of the principals. Bruisers and backers; lords and 'legs'; M.P.'s and mumpers; baronets and beggars; pigeons and rooks—all the country riff-raff and the bucks of St. James behaving so much in accord that only their coats—coloured surtouts or pearl-buttoned Newmarkets—betrayed their differences. Swells, Corinthians, tidy ones, nib-sprigs, bang-up blades, and queer coves—all were there.

There, too, were some who received more attention than the lords. Not only supporters of 'the fancy' were there, but 'the fancy' itself. The giants of the game were there, and small groups followed each one, watching every movement of the great figure, listening to every word dropped by the quiet professional mouth. The huge Tom Cribb was there. The younger Belcher, slim and keen, was there. Little Randall, the whipcord light-weight, was there. The morose Shelton was there. And Tom Spring, magnificent in height and strength and bearing, was there.

Giants they were, and they knew it. Their ambling retinue of lords and commons was one proof of it, and another proof of it was the slim, dark man over there, talking to Lord Windalong: the man who had hailed them as giants and had set their victories in print.

Another observer was there; one who also was to celebrate them and to record their presence at that particular meeting. But him they did not notice. He was a tall, raw-boned youth, and he was talking to a black-curled gipsy wearing a high hat dressed with a peacock's feather. Had they troubled to enquire about him, they would have learned that he was an attorney's clerk, of Norwich, son of Captain Borrow, of the Eastern Counties Militia.

As the champions and their followers moved

across the grass in the bright hubbub, they came from time to time near Lord Windalong, the great patron of the ring. In passing him, hats were touched respectfully. With even greater respect the salutes were returned.

Lord Windalong had just seized upon his companion, the slim, dark man in white cords, top boots, and brown surtout. 'Ha! And here we have the all-accomplished Pierce Egan. No turn-up complete without Pierce Egan.'

'Thank you, my lord. I hope your lordship is in the pink.'

'Yes, indeed. Never felt better. We shall be reading your report of the mill, I s'pose?'

'I hope so, my lord.'

'I warrant the local lad will take a sad drubbing from the big Spraggs.'

'One would say so, my lord, on appearances. But if your lordship can hear a whisper, I would whisper—don't back Spraggs.'

'Not back Spraggs? How? Who could stand against him? Not this clumsy yokel, Fenton?'

'One would think not, my lord. But there are rumours. I say no more.'

'Aha! I smoke you. So! What a cursed thing that corruption should have crept into this manly art.'

'Cursed indeed, my lord.'

'Pray, who is putting forward the yokel?'

'A young man of this district named Thurtell. Well known in the sporting circles of these parts. A would-be blade, my lord. A wide 'un—or thinks so. His father is Mayor of Norwich.'

'So? A respectable money-bags, eh? And this is how the son fattens the bags. The colt is showing the Mayor how to trot, eh, Egan—eh?'

'Good, my lord. Very good. With your lordship's permission, I must book that. I doubt, though, that the colt will trot very far at this pace. They say he talks of settling in London. Certain quarters of London will be glad to see him. As your lordship knows, none is more welcome in those circles than the fly-flat.'

'True, Egan, true. I pity him when the flash coves of Covent Garden have been over him. There'll be little down left on the pigeon then, I fancy.'

'You are in the right, my lord. But in these

quarters he's not the pigeon. He's the other bird. And the London coves are giving him a little wing—so that he will fly to them in time. That's why I say—have a care what you put on the Cockney brave.'

'Thank you, Egan; thank you. If that's the time o' day, I'll not sport my blunt at this meeting. . . . But here comes Goddard with the binders. Good-day, Egan. You must call at Windalong House some noon. I'm looking out for the next number of *Life in London*.'

'Thank you, my lord. I am honoured. Good-day.'

Among the scattered crowd a sudden movement was made towards a particular corner of the heath. From a chaise drawn up on the turf two men were bringing the posts and ropes for the making of the ring. At four separate points look-out men were stationed to keep watch for bailiffs or constables. A thick-set, bull-necked man now forced his way into the crowd. He carried a horse-whip. With this whip he made flourishes round his head. 'Ring! Ring! Make the ring! Clear for the ring!' Under the menace of the lash the crowd fell back. As it fell back, he increased the sweep of the whip, and the crowd fought each other while slowly retreating. Anxiety to escape the flick of the whip was mixed with anxiety to have a front place when the ring should be made. At length, while he kept the whip whirling around him at its full reach, the men with the posts and ropes struggled through the crowd, and the posts were hammered in and the ropes fixed under the control of the ring-master.

Then came the principals and their seconds and their backers. The London man, of huge physique, came first and flung his hat into the ring. He was followed by the local lad, who sent his own hat after the other's. The men went to their corners, and began to strip. Round the ring the mob of flushed and dusty faces became a pudding of face.

The voices of the supporters of each man were heard, and the voices of the 'legs' were heard. 'Two to one—Spraggs.' 'Six to one—Fenton.' 'Ponies?' 'Ponies.' 'Done.' 'Two to one—Spraggs.' 'Do it in hundreds?' 'Yes, hundreds—done.' 'Fenton for ever!' 'Now, Spraggs, lay him out!' 'What about Fenton—lay ten to one against Fenton?' 'I will.' 'Fifties?' 'Fifties—done.' 'What about Spraggs—two to one?' 'Can't do it now, me lord. Evens, Spraggs.' 'All right. Evens. A pony.' 'A pony it is, me lord. Done.'

Time was called. The noise of the crowd faded like a receding wave. It put its being into its eyes. Its eyes centred on the two figures in the ring—the huge, lithe, expert from London, and the windmill bruiser of Norfolk.

Those who had backed the windmill bruiser on faith, felt some dismay as they saw the men shape up. Those who had backed the expert London man felt cheerful. Those who had backed the windmill bruiser from information received, grinned and scarcely followed the moments of the battle.

It did not last long. In the first round the London man sparred. In the second round he fought, and the local windmill began to revolve. In the third round they mixed it, and it was anybody's. In the fourth round, Spraggs came up with all his strength and all his science. The windmill got in a few good ones, but took many more. He was looking groggy. Then, when he was panting and rocking under a terrific jab to the ribs, and the London supporters were cheering-on their man to finish it, a light and undirected blow came out of the windmill, and Spraggs offered it his chin.

Spraggs of London went down. His seconds and the London supporters roared him up. He rolled over. The counting went—'four—five—six—' The Londoners roared, yelled, encouraged, abused. He rested on his hands, head drooping. 'Seven—eight—' His seconds threw a pail of water over him. 'Up—up—come to the count.' 'A flea-bite like that.' 'Thought he was a plucked 'un.' 'Come to the count!' '—nine—ten—Out!'

Cheers from the local party and vicious groans from the Londoners. Hoots and hisses and struggles. 'A cross! A cross! Sold, by God! Rogues! Macers! Sold to the yokels!' Cudgels and whips were brandished. 'He laid down. He laid down—the cursed twicer!'

The London man's body-guard gathered round him. The ring broke up. Cries came from the outskirts—'Who wins? Who wins?'

'Thurtell's man. Fenton. 'Twas a cross. Ay, a cross.' More groans and cheers. Spraggs' guard led him away, followed by an angry tail. Fenton was led away by his backer and his seconds. Hands patted him and voices cheered him. He was on his own soil, and he had won—it didn't matter how. Groups stood around discussing the match. Those who had been at the back listened eagerly for details from those who had had a clear view. These were equally eager to tell. Those who had 'known something' spoke of their winnings as though they were the result of exceptional shrewdness and long sight. They openly pitied those who had not been told anything.

Slowly the crowd dissipated. Amid the clamour of voices the sound of wheels rose and rose. Gigs, chaises and tilburies began to move away towards the city. The common people began to straggle across the heath. Walkers and vehicles, in groups of jubilation or despondency or wrath, went at the same pace because of the press.

Then a sudden change in the aspect of the day made them hasten. Horses were tipped into a trot ; those behind urged those ahead to put on speed. Walkers began to look around for shelter.

The morning, which had been a pure May morning, was now, without a minute's notice, overcast. Up from the south-west had rushed a bank of cloud, blacking out the sun and covering half the sky. Then down came the torrent. There was no gentle preparation of a few heavy drops and a shower. It came at once in full strength. Night was on the heath—night and thunder and hail—all in a few seconds. Fiercer and fiercer fell the rain, and more and more livid became the sky. Its effect was more potent than a posse of constables. The lingering crowd was now a flight. Their dust was washed away. They splashed through mud.

Standing apart from the headlong procession was the tall, raw-boned youth. He was watching it; noting it. To him came the gipsy wearing the peacock's feather. As the gipsy reached him the clouds broke, and became black, purple, yellow and, where the sun touched them, red. The downpour continued, and with it thunder and searing flashes. The gipsy cried something at the ear of the youth.

'I can't hear you, Mr. Petulengro.'

'Brother—do you believe in *dukkeripens*?'

'I do not.'

'I do. Look up there, brother.' The youth looked up. The sky was constantly changing, and at that moment the patches of black, purple, orange and green, had among them a long bright streak of crimson. 'What do you see, brother?'

'A strange kind of cloud.'

'What does it look like, brother?'

'Something like a stream of blood.'

'It foreshoweth a bloody *dukkeripen*.'

'A bloody fortune, eh? And whom may it betide?'

At that moment the crowd in their neighbourhood swiftly split each way, making a lane. Down the lane, scattering the new mud, came a black gig. In it sat two men. One of them was the local victor, Fenton. The other was his backer, a man of athletic appearance, aping the airs of the ring champions but not successfully enough to be taken for one. He wore a Belcher kerchief, a grey Newmarket coat, plush waistcoat, white cords with gold buttons, and a white castor hat. He raised his hat in proud triumph for his man and himself. His face was pale and spotted.

'Whom may it betide?' the gipsy repeated. Then, pointing clear and straight to the man in the gig—'It is *his!*'

II

MR. THURTELL SEEKS LONDON

ON the afternoon following the fight, John Thurtell sat in his Norwich lodgings making plans for the immediate future. The old life was running out and a new life was beckoning. Norwich and the surrounding country were becoming awkward for him. 'Things' were being said, not only about yesterday's fight but about his business default and other matters. The time seemed set for a descent on the larger world of London.

He turned to his companion, his Dearest Fanny, and began to outline the proposed flight.

He sat in an easy chair, wearing a dressing-gown of flowered silk. He was clean-shaven, of tall, lean build, and with stern grey eyes. His hair was brown and short, and his pale face was a little pock-pitted.   He was 'blowing a cloud' from a long Dutch pipe of porcelain and metal. He had a bottle of brandy at his side.   He looked what he wanted to *be*—the complete swell and hail-fellow Corinthian.

Now, if ever, he felt, was the time for a complete break with his native town.   He would go where he knew he would be welcome and would be somebody—not merely the Mayor's son, but a man in his own right.   Free from pious eyes and censorious burgesses.   From a series of discreet bets on yesterday's fight his fortune had risen to some eight hundred pounds. With that he was convinced that he could make a smart entrance on the London stage, and, once there, a man as wide and up to snuff as he was would have no trouble in drawing an easy income. As for Fanny, he wouldn't long be troubled with supporting her.

She was a recent purchase, but already he was tired of her.   Luckily for him and his plans, she was in transports at the idea of London.   She had been reading the monthly parts of Pierce Egan's *Life in London*, and its record of the adventures of the elegant Tom and his cousin Jerry, and she saw herself playing Corinthian Kate to Thurtell's Tom, and sunning herself in her barouche in Rotten Row. Thurtell nourished those dreams, and was very willing that she should accompany him. London was a perfect continent in which to lose the unwanted. Shaking her while he was still living in Norwich would be a matter of difficulty, if not impossible. It would occasion noise and persecution. Also, to go off alone and leave her in Norwich would be to leave an enemy and a source which would feed the flow of dark talk about him, just when it might dry up. By taking her with him he would stop that flow, and somewhere in the labyrinth of strange streets he should easily be able to shake her.

'So, dearest Fanny, we will make it to-night.' His voice was deep, with an engaging ring. 'No time like the present. We will leave at mid-night, and make a two-day journey. In the mean-time, you had better take a rest. We shall be driving through the night.'

'Rest, indeed!' Fanny cried. 'How should a woman rest with London in view? I, who have never seen anything but the dull streets of Norwich and the pursy Quakers and aldermen. Rest! Nay, Jack—no rest for me. I am but too anxious that we should be off. This very minute, if you would but say so.'

'I do not doubt it. But there are one or two small matters I ought to settle first. And as I do not wish to be seen by too many people, I must wait till dark. Then, Fanny, when that little business is done, you and I will be off—to a new life, a free life, a round of interest where dulness cannot enter. And yet I have my misgivings.'

'Misgivings, Jack? But why?'

'I am thinking of you, Fanny.' He was adding a little fire to her excitement, lest she should draw back at the last minute. 'I am thinking of you. For in London, when the bucks and dandies come round you, where will poor Jack be? When Fanny is the toast of White's—the quiz of the opera—the centre of the Row—what use will she have for her old Norfolk friend?'

'Nay, Jack—how you talk. That is not likely to happen to little me, and if it did, do you think there is anybody could displace my Jack from my heart? Why, not His Majesty himself, nor my lord Alvanley, could do that. Believe me, Jack'—and she approached him and took his arm in two hands—'believe me, whoever may desert you, it will not be your Fanny. Though neither has any legal claim on the other—and indeed, I would never seek it—I am yours—yours— yours.'

He put an arm around her and drew her to his knee. 'Indeed, Fanny, I never doubted it. After our first meeting I felt that here was a heart of gold. And I, for my part——'

A sharp knock at the door saved him from a rash affirmation. Fanny started from his knee, and he too got up. Fanny went to the door. He darted into an ante-room leading from the main room. He took his pipe with him; then, looking back, muttered 'Curse the pipe; they'll smell it.' He listened to the talk at the door.

'Two gentlemen asking for Mr. Thurtell.'

'Pray tell them that Mr. Thurtell is in Yarmouth overnight. So many people are seeking him to-day because of the victory of his man at the fight, that he must deny himself. Undesirable people, most of them.'

'Yes, ma'am. These are, too. Leave them to me. I'll send them packing.'

When the door was closed he came out of his retreat, went to the window and peered through the curtains. He turned to Fanny. 'As I thought. That precious rascal, Mosk, has put the bums on me. They've heard I'm in funds over yesterday. Supposed to be my solicitor, and acting all the time for the other side. Decidedly it's time for us to get out. Away from here to some place where things are called by their right names.'

'But why, Jack, are they pursuing you like this?'

'Persecution, my dear. Persecution and roguery. Because I'm the son of the Mayor of Norwich, they think I can be bled, and that the guv'nor will pay up. Believe me, Fanny, in leaving Norwich, I leave with a clear conscience. Lies have been told about me on all sides, but I have nothing with which I can justly reproach myself. I have served my country as a soldier, and in all my dealings afterwards I have observed military honour. Really, though I say it, I am incapable of an unjust or dirty action. But Norwich has been set against me. Nothing has gone right with me in Norwich, and so—farewell Norwich.' He lifted his glass from the side-table. 'Six hours from now we shall, I hope, see it for the last time.'

'And so say I. For surely never was a duller or more horrid hole. And I know you too well to believe that you would ever have done anything that a good sporting blade would not do. What these pot-bellied old merchants judge by, I don't know. But I know that my Jack is superior to all of them.'

'Thank you, Fanny; thank you. It is good to have one true friend to stand by.'

They looked at each other with honest smiles. Thurtell was thinking how clever he was in getting her to London and stopping further scandal in Norwich. Fanny was thinking how lucky she had been in meeting this blade and getting a free passage to the London where she could drop him and make her fortune. Here, as throughout his life, Thurtell was the unawares flat.

'Tell me,' she went on, ' shall we, on the way up to London, pass through Hertford?'

'Hertford? No; I don't recollect that as on our road. Why do you ask?'

'I have a curiosity to see Hertford. A very dear aunt of mine left here some years ago and settled at Hertford. I would much like to see her, but if that is impossible I would like to see the town where she lives.'

'No; it's not on our route, I'm sure. And I've heard that it's a very dull town. Nothing ever happens there, any more than here. I've never seen it and have no wish to. Still, if it would gratify you, Fanny, we could go out of our way.'

'Oh, no. Pray do not think of it. I only thought that if it was in our way I would like to see it. But do not let us do anything to delay our approach to London—where, I am sure, we are both going to be happy. London is our goal. Hertford, I am sure, can have nothing for you or for me.'

'Not while there's such a city as London, I hope.'

21

'Indeed, no. Fancy—there are people who live and die in Norwich, and know nothing of anything outside it. How truly pitiful—ending one's days in a place like this. Or a place like Hertford.'

'Pitiful it is. Still, if you want to see Hertford, I——'

'No, Jack. The direct way to London. And as quickly as possible.'

'With all my heart. And doubtless we shall both die happy without ever seeing Hertford. But come—have you packed all that you will require?'

'Yes, everything. I have only to change my outer dress and put on a travelling hood, and I am ready at any hour.'

'That's my Fanny speaking. You're the right woman for a sporting man. These simpering misses and agitated matrons raise my spleen. Give me the girl who's a man's girl. Ready for anything. The brazen hussy is my sort, and that's the sort you are. Dare and do, and devil take—eh?'

'That's the time o' day, Jack.'

'Aha! Zounds! Wait till we're in London. You'll be a quick learner, Fanny.' She flew to his arms. They embraced. Then, gently setting her aside, he said: 'Well, now; I see it's dusk. I'll just slip out and settle one or two things I have to settle—with the few friends I have left— and then I'll be back. I've ordered the gig for just after eleven. And then—London!'

'London!' Fanny echoed, clasping him.

.   .   .   .   .

John Thurtell, the would-be blade, the mixed bluffer and flat, was not a bad man. He had no driving tendency to good or bad, but at twenty-seven he was drifting to bad. The kind of life which appealed to him—the life of which the Prince Regent had been the exemplar—had its being on a bad road; a road which only the man of positive good force can safely ride. Under good management Thurtell might have been a negatively decent man. Riding this road, he became, by stages imperceptible to himself, a desperate, but still not a positive, bad man.

His was a situation that repeats itself often—

23

the son of the wealthy, respectable merchant, getting his head at too early an age, mixing with a livelier class than his own, and revolting against citizen prudence and citizen manners. By twenty-five he had been both soldier and sailor, and had seen action in Spain. On retiring from the Army, he placated his father by going into business. But he took into business the easy style and manners of the officers' mess and the betting ring.

He was not long in learning that Corinthianism and business are not good partners; and only a little longer in finding his enterprises sunk in disaster. His faults in the matter were the faults of an expansive nature and a trusting habit—the 'flat' side of him, which made him fair game to the end of his short life. He made the mistake of treating business-men as though they were betting-men.

He had learned on the turf and at the ring-side that a bet was a bet. A word, a nod, confirmed it. No paper was needed. The leg's word was gold. He followed this form in business, and thought that as a business-man was so much more respectable than a betting-man, therefore a business-man's word could be trusted even beyond a leg's. He was not the first to discover that levanting and shady dealings are rather more common in respectable commerce than in disreputable rings and enclosures.

He was now celebrating this discovery by an abrupt retreat from his troubles and by turning to a world he understood; a world where crossing was called crossing, and Greeking was called Greeking, and neither was called Business. The respectable world of commerce had given him the first push along that road which was to end for him at Hertford.

. . . . .

At eleven o'clock, when all the streets were still, Fanny heard the wheels of a gig. Throwing on a cloak and hood, and catching up a muff, she met Thurtell as he ran up the stairs.

'All's in order,' he said, 'and the coast clear. Give me your basket.' He threw off his surtout, and replaced it with a heavy, three-caped box-coat; then picked up the basket, and a small leather case of his own, and looked round the

room. 'What's left here in the way of clothes
I've told my brother Thomas to send for, and
dispose as he pleases. We can replenish in
London. There's nothing else, I think. Have
you taken all you want to take?'

'Yes, all.'

'Then let's lose no more time.'

They went swiftly down the stairs and out to
the street. Without fuss, or modest arranging
of her skirts, Fanny climbed into the black gig.
Thurtell followed. He took up the reins, gave
a touch to his ' bit of blood,' and they were off.
They went along Tombland, through the Market
Place, and then turned to the Newmarket Road—
the road for London. In a few minutes they were
off the stones of Norwich and free from the
troubles and tedium of a city which neither
wished to see again.

Southward through the blue night went Mr.
Thurtell and his gig. Within less than three
years he and his gig were to come to the notice
of a Scottish philosopher who, by Mr. Thurtell's
unawares help, was to add a new word to the
language. Going along that turnpike road under

the stars, Mr. Thurtell was already in process of helping the dictionary to its new word.

But of that he knew nothing. He knew only that he was rid of Norwich; that he would soon be rid of Fanny; and that before him lay London and a genial career of ring and course and green-baize table. He was never to hear the word which would for ever be associated with his name—*Gigmanity*.

III

EAGER as Mr. Thurtell was to get to London, the town, as Pierce Egan had suggested, was equally eager for his arrival.

There had been those at the Mousehold Heath fight, knowing ones, who had observed this flash provincial blade, and had brought home news of him. He was just the stuff that made the daily bread of their sort—the lower ranks of the Sporting Gents. In Norwich they had enquired about him, and all that they had heard confirmed their summing-up of his half-baked 'wideness.' They deplored the fate that kept this rich lump of ore among the yokels. They prayed that something might happen that should deliver it, unworked, into their hands. They cast about for schemes and ruses which would bring it to London.

Then, while they were debating the trapping of the pigeon, their prayer was granted. The word passed that it was flying straight into their hands.

Secret as his departure from Norwich had been it was not so secret as he thought. By those strange and impalpable means of acquiring and communicating knowledge which sporting circles possess, news had reached London that he was coming. Before he had passed a dozen toll-gates it was known in the Strand and in Covent Garden that he was on his way. And it was spoken as a certainty that, being the kind of man he was, he would put up at the Piazza Coffee House, over-looking the Market. Scouts were ordered to watch for his coming.

.   .   .   .   .

On Wednesday afternoon following the Monday midnight, he and Fanny were within rumour of London. They were coming along the Essex approach to it.

On that same afternoon the back room of the Brown Bear, in Bow Street, was preparing to receive company. It was two o'clock, and the room was laid for entertaining certain gentlemen during the hours before their dinner-time—five o'clock. Round the green table a lonely figure wandered; a short, sallow, black-bearded man of about forty. From time to time he picked up a dice-box and rattled the bones, and made experimental throws; or amused himself by shuffling and reshuffling a pack of cards, with certain dexterous twists which brought required cards to required places.

This black-bearded fellow, who had rooms in Lyon's Inn, was of no occupation than that afforded by the card-table and the ring-side, from which he made a comfortable living. He was waiting for the arrival of a few cronies with whom he would shake the elbow or flip the broads. He was also waiting for the arrival of Mr. John Thurtell, of whom he had heard. He was waiting, too, though he did not know it, for death. The one gig was bringing both.

So shake the elbow and flip the broads, William Weare. You have not many months left for your favourite play. Make the most of them. Play on. Those cards in your hands are death's visiting-cards. Mr. Thurtell's black gig is now a mere twenty miles distant from you. Every hour brings it nearer. Even as you rise to greet your cronies, Mr. Thurtell has baited his horse at Harlow, and the wheels of his gig are turning rapidly over the last miles of the road from East Anglia to London—and to you.

.   .   .   .   .

With noise and swagger the flash friends of Mr. Weare turned in at the door of the Brown Bear, and with noise and swagger greeted the land-lord. With noise and swagger increased by the confined space they swept through the bar-parlour into the farther room, and greeted Weare. People not well-informed in the grades of London society might have taken them for Corinthian swells. They were in fact the pinchbeck version of the swell and the pinchbeck version of the Crockford gamester. They were of that rank of pretender known as Flash Coves.

The landlord in the doorway announced them. 'Here's Mr. Lemon and Mr. Cox, sir.' Lemon

31

and Cox, in Newmarket coats and tall beavers, came in, followed by a third man—a stout, well-built fellow in specially dandy dress and luxuriant whiskers, and with a coarse confidence. Behind the trio, loose and dowdy by contrast with the general flashiness, came two or three of their hangers-on and toadies.

Weare greeted his two friends with an un-smiling face, and cried perfunctory halloas to them. 'Ah, my dear Bill,' cried Lemon; and the tone was indeed a cry; 'here we are, you see. Right on the hour.' He brought forward the third man. 'Let me have the pleasure of present-ing to you a good friend of mine—Mr. Joe Hunt, the celebrated vocalist of Vauxhall and the Coal Hole—Mr. Weare.'

'It is a pleasure indeed,' said Weare, 'to welcome Mr. Hunt to our circle. His name is by no means unknown to me.' Hunt bowed. Weare offered his snuff-box, and each took a pinch. 'Come, lads,' he went on, 'let's cut for blind hookey. But first let's wet. Here— Crawford!' He hailed the landlord. 'Bring glasses, and some of your best Madeira for my friends. And give the boys there some max or heavy—or whatever they want. Well, Lemon, what's the time o' day? Cox—you give me my revenge this afternoon, don't you? I think the devil was in the cards on Monday. Here's Crawford with the Old Bual. Prime stuff it is, too. Come—fill up, and what news?' He said all this with a strict, expressionless face.

They drank and smacked their tongues. 'News?' said Cox, in a harsh tone. 'News? Surely, Weare, you should have more than we. The Inns of Court should provide plenty, I fancy. Don't you learn at Lyon's Inn what terms the Earl and Countess are coming to over the little milliner? Ain't you had a sight of the pleas in the new *crim. con.* case?'

'Pah!' Weare made a coarse gesture. 'Such stuff. as that. The mere small change of news. Let's have some real news. Have no new mugs rattled into town lately?'

'None that I hear of,' said Lemon. 'Save, perhaps, my good friend Hunt here.'

There was a general loud laugh. Hunt dug Lemon in the ribs. 'You quiz me, my dear

Lemon. Would that I could deserve it. Would that I could be again as innocent as I once was. Before I met you.'

'Nay,' said Weare, 'I fear we have nothing to hope for from Mr. Hunt. From all I have heard of him, he has long been all the go and up to the sharps.'

'I was well instructed,' said Hunt modestly, with a leer at Lemon.

'But what was Cox telling us yesterday,' said Weare, 'of the dumpling from Norfolk. Was he not arriving? Or has he been decoyed on the way?'

Cox laughed. 'No, indeed. He ain't yet arrived, but he'll be here before long. We ain't lost sight of him by a long chalk. And when he does arrive, we shall know. One of the lads'— he indicated the shabby group drinking at another table—'will give us the office. And then we must nobble him.'

'Ah, yes. You have as yet no plan, I suppose?'

'Well, you, Weare, I think, would be the most suitable to welcome the little stranger to the great city, and steer him through its perils. You are the most personable, and you have the disarming countenance of Everybody's Good-Natured Friend. Yes, when we have the word, and know his hotel, I certainly think that you, better than any of us, could scrape acquaintance with him without suspicion. We fellows look too much like what we are.'

'With all my heart,' said Weare. 'Does he lush?'

'Like a fish, I'm told.'

'Good. And is he really a prize?'

'Well, I don't know. But I've heard talk of seven or eight hundred.'

'H'm. Not a gold mine, exactly. Still, every little helps. And it's a deal of tin for a country sport. He ought not to be trusted with it. Somebody ought to mind it for him, in case it's taken off him by some of these Greeks. Eh? Aha!'

'Yes,' said Hunt, who had been listening attentively. 'And don't you think, Mr. Weare, that the way to do it is this—for *you* to be the flat, and let *him* show you the town? Eh? You be the mug not up to the tricks, and let him

Lure You On to play? And lose a bit. Then you've got him. Eh?'

Weare considered. 'Yes. Good. Very good. Mr. Hunt is a man of ideas. These wide-o boys always like to help the innocent. Yes, we'll work it that way. I'll be the solemn citizen, who's never seen life. Would rather like to, but shrinks from it, not knowing his way about. That's the idea. Thank you, Mr. Hunt.'

Faster and faster went the wheels of Mr. Thurtell's gig as he approached London and glory by way of Woodford and Leyton. Mr. Weare could not hear them. While he was chuckling at the thought of his playing the mug, he could not know that later he was actually to be the mug of Mr. Thurtell and of the celebrated vocalist, and to be lured to Elstree in Mr. Thurtell's gig. Nor could the celebrated vocalist know that that afternoon marked the first step towards landing him at the convict colony of New South Wales.

They were a group of merry fellows planning a little lark of the kind which was being worked every week in that part of the town—and nothing said by anybody. Each of them had been through the process of being fleeced, and each of them had accepted it with a shrug, and worked it on the next newcomer. Had they been told that they were villains, they would not have understood. Nor would they have understood any victim bearing malice. They had not so far run against the dour and revengeful type. They did not know their John Thurtell.

'Yes,' said Weare again, 'that's the idea. And now let's have a sitting. Pray, Mr. Hunt, will you shuffle?'

They sat to the table, and, as Hunt shuffled, and as each man cut, all eyes were alert. There were no mugs here. They knew the tricks, and they wouldn't trust any friend's fingers out of sight. And they declined to be drawn into conversation. Conversation they knew as a means of distracting the necessary concentration.

During the game men of their own sort strolled in and out. Some stood and watched their play. Some set up tables of their own.

It was a long, low room, stale of odour, with tarnished candelabra, dull mirrors, and soiled carpet. The walls were adorned with prints of

Broughton, Slack, and earlier heroes of the ring; prints of cock-fights; plates of notable horses. It held an atmosphere of determined hilarity, but the only truly cheerful face to be seen was that of the landlord. The faces of the others were keen and set. His was affable and bland. He did not play.

Moving from one parlour to another he came to the door of the card-room and looked over the shabby group who had accompanied Lemon and Cox. He picked on one of them. 'Dick, here's a cove outside asking for you.'

Dick got up and shuffled out. Within a minute he came back and went towards the card-table, and made a noise at Lemon. 'Sst! Your gent's here.'

'Ha! At the Piazza?'

'No. At the Hummums.'

Lemon, sitting at the bank, grinned at the others. 'Now for some sport, my merry lads. Weare—the luck's been with you this afternoon. Let's hope it holds for you with the Norfolk Dumpling.'

IV

SOME months after his introduction to the Brown
Bear, Mr. Joseph Hunt, the celebrated vocalist
from Vauxhall Gardens and the Coal Hole, was
bowing to the applause following his final encore—
'Bright chanticleer proclaims the dawn.'   He had
just reached the side of the platform in a farewell bow, when his eye was caught by another
eye.

He was at the Argyll Rooms that night, and the
eye that caught his was that of his friend Lemon.
Passing from the platform he came out to the
hall in his cloak, and while a new performer was
engaging public attention he approached Lemon.
Lemon took his arm, and they went out together.

In the dark street they thrust aside the offers
of the link-boys and the coach-touts, and turned

into a side street near Golden Square, where it was still darker. Hunt said, 'Well?'

Lemon said: 'Weare's got the Norfolk Dumpling at last. Had rather a job of it. Thurtell's been so occupied. Been dabbling in business. Fairly successfully, too. Had a drapery business in his brother's name, and the place was burned down. He collected a couple of thousand on that, but the insurance people don't like it. They say it was a plant, and they're looking into it. However, with the money he's set his brother up as landlord of The Cock, in Haymarket. That's his headquarters now. That's where Weare nobbled him, and the flat's promised to take Weare to Kerrigan's in Shire Lane, and show him a bit of life. The talk is, he's down to three hundred pounds, and hopes to double it on Weare. I s'pose you'd like to be in it?'

'I should be hurt if I were left out,' Hunt said, and so took one more step towards New South Wales.

'It's to-morrow night, then. Seven. At Kerrigan's.'

'I'll be there, trust me. Where are you for now?'

'I was going Drury Lane way.'

'I'm for that direction, too. I was going to look in at Oxberry's—the Craven's Head, to see a pal or two.'

'Ah, yes—your professional house.'

'Or the Temple of Thespis, as we call it. Give me your company, and take a look at us.'

'I'm your man,' Lemon said; and they went slowly through the faintly-lit streets of Westminster under the recently introduced gas-light.

.   .   .   .   .

Next evening they met at Kerrigan's. They got there before seven, but Cox was already there. The three of them, with two of their hangers-on, took a table and began to play a casual and no-stakes game. 'If they see us playing,' Lemon said, 'Weare may be able to get Thurtell to suggest sitting-in with us.'

Two or three other tables were occupied by players with dice or cards, but Lemon contrived, by a little acting, to make their table quietly conspicuous to newcomers.

Soon after seven they saw Weare come in to

the parlour with the Swell Yokel—the name London had given him. Weare played his part well. The Swell Yokel, looking half bruiser, half jockey, entered with an air of self-possession, as of one familiar with all London ways and with all haunts of this kind, high and low. Weare entered with a touch of nervousness, which he tried to cover. He kept close to his companion. He looked about him with an affected careless-ness. Any outside observer would have said that here was the simple city sprig, seeing life for the first time. The carelessness was overdone; the quite-at-ease air was awkwardly worn. Behind Thurtell's back he caught the eyes of his friends at their table. He kept his face wooden.

Thurtell gave his order for a bottle of sherry and glasses in a peremptory tone. He let it be seen that he knew his way about, and was not to be put upon. The waiter was obsequious. His customer suggested that with him it was two words and a blow. The sherry and glasses appeared in quick time. Thurtell filled the glasses, and future murderer and future victim drank to each other.

Thurtell set down his glass with a crack. 'Curse the women!'

Weare raised his eyebrows. 'You suffer in that way, sir?'

'Suffer! Rot me—if one considered the women as much as they expect to be considered, one would never have a moment's pleasure. Every evening it's the same. One only has to say that one's going out for a spree—and then they talk of neglect. They have our days—and our nights —and they want our evenings as well. However, I'm done with them now. Or shall be by to-morrow night.'

'Troublesome,' said Weare. 'Very. For myself I have no entanglements of that nature. My hours are my own. Two hours is as much of my company as any woman has. And never the same woman—aha!'

'You have a wise head,' said Thurtell. 'I was a fool. But somehow these spells come on one, and one makes an alliance—or a misalliance. And it's not easy to end. Though I've found a means which I think will work. You like this Manzanilla?'

'A little thin, don't you think? I thought men drank full-bodied tipple in these places?'

'Thin? Nay, sir. Delicate, if you will, but not thin. But I see how it is. Like most of the inexperienced, you want to set the pace hot and fast. Moderation, sir; moderation. All tempests begin slowly. A prime place this, ain't it?'

'It is, indeed. Just the kind of place I have always wanted to see. I observe they are at play in the next room. Do they play high here, do you know?'

'Just as it goes, according to the party. They please themselves. What say you to shaking an elbow? A foolish thing, in my view, but 'pon my life London's so cursed slow these days, there's little else to do.'

'What was that game we played the other night?'

'That? Oh, ah—you did well at that. It's called blind hookey. Were I in Government, it would be abolished. 'Tis the curse of the town.'

'Well, as you say, there's little else to do. And so long as we don't play high, I'm your man for a cut. Isn't that the game the gentlemen over there are playing?'

'Yes. They're at blind hookey.'

'Why, they look a quiet and respectable group. Do you think they would allow us to join? I have heard that is a custom in some of these places.'

'Oh, indeed, yes. Quite general.' Thurtell looked them over, and they were playing so sedately that he decided that he had lighted upon a useful group of mugs. 'Yes. Do you, if you will, approach them and ask them. Your appearance will disarm any suspicion they might have of strangers. I, perhaps, look a little too sporting for their taste.'

Weare got up and approached the group. His face, as he met their glances, was blank. Strangers in the room would have sworn that he was unacquainted with them. But one was present who was aware of the group and of Weare's link with them.

Sitting solitary at a table with a bottle of claret was a slim fellow with a shrewd mouth. He had been eyeing Weare and Thurtell under pretence of holding his glass to the light, and had been watching the little comedy. He had seen it played many times, but this form of the decoy being supposedly led to the slaughter by the victim was a new twist. With a private grin he saw Weare go timidly and courteously towards his old cronies; then he finished his claret, got up, and strolled out.

As he passed Thurtell, who was awaiting the return of Weare from the table, he stooped and adjusted his Wellingtons. From the side of his mouth he muttered: 'Have a care, sir. Have a care.' As he straightened up, he patted his pocket and jerked his head towards the gang's table.

Thurtell looked up with a haughty stare. Then gave a rude laugh. 'Impudent puppy! Don't know who you're talking to, I fancy. Pious prig, ain't you?' The man passed on and out. Thurtell followed him with a hard stare. But the man did not turn. Rescuing flats was no mission of his, but on occasions, when he saw young men in company whose sort they did not know, this wanderer was kindly enough to drop a word. The word here, as at most other times, fell unheeded.

Thurtell sipped his sherry, and gave a scornful chuckle at the idea of his being warned against fast company. Him, the Go of the Goes. Doubtless the fellow was some poor clerk who had once lost one of his master's guineas in this room. On Weare's beckoning to him, he forgot about the fellow. The man with the shrewd mouth did not forget about Thurtell. During his wanderings about London, he heard of him, and occasionally saw him. They did not meet again to exchange conversation until a year later, when the man visited Hertford Gaol for that express purpose.

Acknowledging Weare's signal he went across to the table, and thereby moved a little closer to the doom which his conceited flatness was preparing. 'These gentlemen,' said Weare, 'are quite agreeable to our sitting-in.'

Thurtell bowed. 'Thank you, gentlemen. My name is Thurtell. My friend's name is Weare. Two persons of no celebrity at present; but we are young yet, and who knows?'

The men at the table greeted the sally with

polite smiles. Lemon spoke. 'My name is Lemon. This gentleman is Mr. Cox. And this is Mr. Hunt—a gentleman who *is* a celebrity—in London at least. Mr. Joe Hunt is a vocalist of great renown. And may yet be known beyond London.'

Thurtell again bowed. 'But who would wish to be known beyond London? What is the worth of renown among yokels? To be known in London is surely the crown of every man's ambition.'

'True. But Mr. Hunt enjoys fame, and can always take more. Indeed, he can take as much fame as Tom Spring can punishment. He has no objection to being known all over England. Have you, Hunt?'

Hunt grinned. Thurtell said, 'Then I trust his ambition will be gratified.' They looked at each other.

Did any interior corner of their being register a recognition? Did they, in some nerve-cell, know that Hunt's wish and Thurtell's hope for it, would be fulfilled? Did they, somewhere in the last recesses of their god-selves, realise that

48

all their previous progress had been leading them to this meeting? Their faces did not show it; but the momentary separation of the two, and the effacing of Lemon, Cox, and Weare, made a tiny link. Each felt that something had happened. Some little pulse or emanation of each man conveyed to the mind of the other—'We two are of a kind.'

And Weare? Did he feel no whisper of the blood in that moment of introducing to the circle his destroying angel? His face was blank. He was a clod. The unseen and the unheard could not penetrate his earth. On the sound-waves of a year hence, waiting for time to reach and release them, certain syllables were faintly throbbing. Syllables that made a verse, which all England was to know:

> They cut his throat from ear to ear ;
> His brains they battered in.
> His name was Mr. William Weare ;
> He lived at Lyon's Inn.

But had their throbbing been at thunder-strength his clogged nerves would not have heard them.

E   49

Play began.   The bank fell to Weare.   Thurtell
hid a chuckle.   That night his devil was born.

  •   •   •   •   •

Five hours later he was not chuckling.

After five hours' play, three hundred pounds
had gone from his pocket to Weare's.

And he could make no complaint.   Nothing
he had seen in the play—and he had kept his eyes
skinned and his senses alert—could be labelled
'macing.'   And yet he knew that he had been
'maced.'   He knew by something in the air that
the game had been rigged from the start, and was
a plant.

When he rose from the table his pale face wore
an angry red.   He looked down at the men.
'Rigged—eh?   Those cards were stacked.'

'Stacked, sir?'

'Yes, by Gard—stacked.   Weare, you worked
this.'

'I, sir?   I?   Why, I myself lost heavily at one
time.'

'Of course.   Part of the rigging.   You're in
with this gang, and you worked me for them.'

'Have a care what you say, sir,' said Lemon. 'Accusing sporting gentlemen of——'

'Sporting gentlemen me eye. There's nothing of *Sporting* or of *Gentleman* about any of you. A pack of thimble-riggers. Weare—I know you worked this. But you worked it on the wrong man this time. My last three hundred!' His voice remained deep but rose in strength.

'Come, sir, come.' The other men got up. Thurtell's tall, athletic figure, and the clenching of his fist, gave them some concern. ' Come, now,' Lemon said. 'All's square with us boys. You can have your revenge some other time. And you can sit in with us when we find another pigeon.'

'You admit it, then. And I can have my revenge, can I? Then I shall take it. Be sure of that. But not, perhaps, in the way you think. The man sitting over there was right. This was a plant. And Weare was your decoy. The slinking hound!' The men looked at Weare, but he remained stolid under the insult. 'I'll let the town know your sort. I'll spread this.'

Weare answered quietly: 'You dare not.

You yourself are a fraud. All the town knows the insurance people are after Jack Thurtell. And what about buying the knuckle fight at Norwich?'

'Damn your eyes for a——' He took a step towards Weare. The other three put themselves between them. Thurtell looked at them. His eyes held the intention of wiping the floor with them; and they felt that he could do it. Then he shook his shoulders. 'Very well. There will be another time. Mark this, William Weare —I never forget.'

Weare looked at him with a sneer. 'You forget *yourself*, Thurtell.'

Thurtell spat on the floor at their feet. 'Pah!' With a swing of the arms he turned and strode out. He had not only lost all he had. Weare's taking him in by posing as a flat had wounded him in a sensitive spot—his vanity. Whoever wounded him there made an implacable enemy.

    ·   ·   ·   ·   ·

When he reached the Strand the nightwatch-men, with lanterns and rattles, were setting out from St. Clement's Watch House. The night was deeply dark, with a high wind. He buttoned his long blue coat, and pressed against the wind towards Haymarket. A few uproarious bucks passed him, reeling and singing. He heard the urgent summons of rattles. Dashing Cyprians sauntered by, ogling and chaffing. One couple accosted him, and then cried together: 'Why, it's Jack Thurtell.' And one said: 'Our generous protector. Nobody's in front of Jack Thurtell when it comes to real gemmen.'

The compliment pleased him. It smoothed away the ruffles of the affair at Kerrigan's. He stopped and smiled. 'Sorry, my dears, but Jack can't do anything to-night. Cleaned out. Cleaned out by a pack of ruffians at Kerrigan's.'

'What—Jack Thurtell cleaned out? But you're up to everything.'

'Yes. But this wasn't by assault, which I can deal with. Or by the regular tricks, which I know. It was a new kind of crossing.'

'Well, there's always something new in this town. One has to be up early and late to learn it all.'

'Ever heard of a man named William Weare?'

'Yes, he lives close by. Just here—at Lyon's Inn. Why?'

'He was the cadger that worked it.'

'Oh, we know him. Know him well. He's a bilker. A money-bags. Takes all that a poor girl has, and then gets out of it by threatening to charge you with robbing him if you don't go away. That's his sort. Hoarding up the dibs is all he cares for. And getting them any way he can.'

'Thanks for the information, my dears. Well, one of these days, the Strand will be rid of Mr. William Weare. And you'll thank me. Meantime—another night, perhaps. When I'm in funds. God bless you.'

He walked on, but he did not get far before he was stopped again. He had almost reached the end of Holywell Street when he heard a voice which said 'Thurtell! Thurtell!' He stopped and stepped into a doorway, and turned from the wind, preparing himself for conflict with bailiffs. 'It's Hunt. Joe Hunt.'

'Indeed! One of the precious gang. Well,

I've got nothing more on me. And if I had you wouldn't get it here. There's plenty alleys round here, if that's your game. And if you want to be found in one of 'em.'

Hunt softened his voice. 'One of the gang, as you say. And you may shake me off, if you will. I have no wish to force myself upon you. But—well, I've taken a liking to you. And I just wanted to tell you that you were right in your surmise. The game *was* a plant. And the cards *were* stacked. In a new way. Weare invented the way, and it hasn't been blown yet.'

Thurtell growled. 'I thought it must be new. Nobody's ever crossed Jack Thurtell at cards yet.'

'Yes. Weare's mighty clever at that kind of thing. I just thought I'd like to warn you to keep away from the gang. I'm not fond of their company myself. But at present I'm not flush—short of the blunt—my profession ain't what it was—and I have to pick up where I can without being too particular.'

'Thanks for the warning,' Thurtell said. 'A little late, don't you think? But no matter for that. I'm not taking it. I'm not going to keep away from the gang. I'm going to cultivate them because I'm going to get back on that William Weare.' He bawled this and spat.

'Well,' Hunt said, 'that's for you. I've told you what they are. And, as I say, I've taken a liking to you.' He walked beside Thurtell, a stout, dark figure, overtopped by the other, and taking three steps to keep up with Thurtell's two.

Thurtell, looking straight ahead, spoke automatically; and, not quite knowing why he said it, said: 'Well, I've no special grievance against *you*. It's Weare I'm riled with. The dirty, double-crossing son of a——'

'Yes. Weare's not much liked by any of us. He's been one too many for quite a lot of people. He got me that way on my first meeting him. But he'll find his account one day.'

'And before very long, believe me. He'll pay handsomely for this. Just when I was in need of cash to meet certain troubles. And worse—fooling me in that way. I look forward to another merry meeting with him.'

'Well, you'll find him most mornings at Rexworthy's Billiards Room, in Spring Gardens. And in the afternoons at the Brown Bear, Bow Street.'

'I am obliged.   Which way do you go?'

'I was making for my lodgings—just off Golden Square.'

'Then you would be taking Haymarket in your way.   Pray stop a few moments at my place, The Cock.'

'This is indeed kind of you.   After what has passed.'

'Not at all.   It occurs to me that we might, I don't know how, be of use each to the other. Things turn up from time to time.   Will you come?'

'With the greatest pleasure.'

.   .   .   .   .

Hunt had indeed taken a liking to Thurtell, and their brief conversation increased it.   He himself didn't like Weare, and had no great opinion of Cox and Lemon.   Thurtell's figure and manner appealed to him.   He seemed, if a little more brutal, at any rate a little cleaner than these others. Hunt was no hero, and had never thought of tackling Weare, or even of expressing his dislike. He was glad therefore to meet a man who seemed ready to tackle the fellow. Like most men who are no heroes, he instinctively recognised and respected the hero in others. And he had recognised in Thurtell the bold blade, fearless of God and of any man and any law. He felt that he would like to know Thurtell.

When they arrived at The Cock, in the middle of the west side of Haymarket, and passed down the hall, they were greeted with cries. Thurtell had such an 'entrance' and reception as Hunt had at the Coal Hole. From the various rooms and the drinking parties at the bars came thick voices: 'Here's Jack. Here's Old Flare. Whoa there, Jack!' Thurtell, who was usually pleased by this toadying, acknowledged it to-night with curt nods; he was thinking of his three hundred pounds. He pushed through the throng, and led the way upstairs. Hunt followed him. At the top of the stairs a waiter met him. 'Mr.

Probert's here, with some other gentlemen. In the blue room.'

In the blue room they found three men sitting at a table. Glasses and a bottle of rum were on the table. Probert, a thick-set, broad-faced Welshman, gave a grunt to Thurtell and a suspicious glance to Hunt. Thurtell presented him. 'Mr. Joe Hunt, the celebrated singer, of Vauxhall and other gay spots. Three friends of mine— Mr. Probert, Mr. Wood, Mr. Noyes. Mr. Hunt is one of us. A choice spirit.'

Wood smiled. 'Ah! Mr. Hunt's name is well known. Perhaps he will tip us a stave. Perhaps he knows a rum chant or two?'

Hunt bowed. 'Great pleasure, gentlemen. And I certainly do know one or two songs not quite suitable for Vauxhall. And one which I would hesitate to do even at the Cyder Cellar.'

'Bravo!' they cried. 'Prime fellow. Sit down.'

Thurtell drew chairs for his guest and himself, and they joined the table. 'Probert—put the bottle round.' They clinked glasses. The trio who were to become as widely known as even

Hunt could have desired—Thurtell, Hunt, and Probert—had met. Thurtell, fulfilling his destiny as the half-awake flat, had just introduced the two men who were to save their necks by betraying him.

Mr. William Weare was lying serenely asleep in Lyon's Inn.

V

MR. THURTELL HAS TO RUN

A MONTH or so later, in January 1823, John
Thurtell, having wandered down Haymarket from
The Cock, found himself near Spring Gardens.
The name awoke a little unsettled matter which
was waiting for attention at the side of his mind.
He had picked up a hundred or so, and was ready
for revenge. His devil was itching.

He turned into Spring Gardens and into
Rexworthy's Billiards Room. He strolled up
and down the room, casting his eye here and
there. Then he saw his man talking to Rexworthy.

He went casually towards them. Weare,
seeing him coming, at first avoided his eye; but
as he kept it fixed, it was finally met. Thurtell
said: 'Morning.' Weare returned the greeting.

Thurtell nodded to the tables. 'You play the game?' Weare said he did.

'Ah! Well, after that affair at Shire Lane, you offered me my revenge. What do you say— shall we play?'

'I'm your man.'

'Fifty on the game?'

'As you please. Hundred if you like.'

'Hundred it is. And let me tell you I choose this game because billiard balls can't be stacked.'

'That comes ill from Jack Thurtell.'

'Worse things may come yet. When others play me fair, I play fair. When others cross, I cross. This game is open. I'll take on you or any other man at this—if he was the biggest Greek.'

'You have confidence in your skill.'

'I have. I back it. If a better man beats me, I've been beaten—not cheated. Do you break?'

'Very well.'

They went to the table. And Thurtell's pride in his own prowess again broke him. Always, it seemed, he was to make his own trouble (and eventually his own end) as the unawares flat.

Nobody in Norfolk could have touched him at billiards. But in seeking revenge of Weare he had, by neglecting to inform himself of Weare's ability, selected a man who was a 'prime hand' with the cue—the primest in London. Weare's first break was thirty-five. Thurtell cursed him. He went to the table and made a miscue. He cursed the cue and the balls and the table. Weare made another twelve. While he was making it Thurtell took a brandy. When he went to the table the second time he ran to thirty-two. Weare made a three, and left the balls well placed for Thurtell. Thurtell looked at them, and round the table, and looked at Weare.

'Double it?'

'If you will. Two hundred pounds on the hundred up.'

Thurtell snapped 'No! Two hundred guineas.'

'Two hundred guineas it is.'

Thurtell went cautiously to the table and studied the lie of the balls for some seconds. He made a break of twenty-eight. He permitted himself a thin smile.

Four minutes later the smile was gone. Weare had run out to his hundred, still in play.

Thurtell flung the cue to the floor. 'By Gard—rot you!'

'Two hundred guineas, Thurtell, at your convenience. And this time, as you said, you can have no complaint of—er—stacking.'

'I grant that. But I had not thought that Mr. Weare was proficient in extracting money by so many and various talents.'

'Well, well. We live and learn, Thurtell. We live and learn. One should always know one's man before one plays any kind of game with him. Keep that in mind.'

'I want no advice from you.'

'Yet you would do well to take it.' He picked up the notes which Thurtell had flung to the table, and unfastened his under-coat, and unfastened his shirt. From under the shirt he drew a leather bag. In opening it and adding his new winnings he disclosed a mass of notes and an assortment of gold. Thurtell stared. Weare gave a cunning nod. He had no fear of this poor flat, Jack Thurtell. 'My bank.

Never travel without it. Never at a loss to pay out.'

Thurtell, still frowning at his loss and at seeing it go into this bulging bag, said 'Dangerous.' And thought : ' You won't have that long.'

'No,' said Weare. 'Can't be snatched. Can't be cut. Secret attachment. Patent lock. And I never go home by dark streets.' He put the last of the notes in, snapped the lock, replaced it under his shirt, buttoned his coat—and smiled. Then he tapped Thurtell on the arm.

'And now, my good fellow, fair's fair. I've won from you and I'm willing you should win from me. Luck was against you to-day—and before. But as a sporting man you deserve to win. I like you. And as a sporting man I'll let you in on something.' Weare had no desire to lose this agreeable bird by winning too much from him. There might be other pickings to come from that nest. 'I'll let you in on something. There's a knuckle fight coming on in Hertfordshire—at Wade's Mill. We're all in it, and you——'

At the word 'fight' Thurtell was off his guard.

His face lit up. 'Indeed? I love the ring. I love to be among the men of the Fancy.'

'You shall. And more.' He offered his snuff-box. After a moment's hesitation Thurtell took a pinch and listened. 'One of the men is ours. He's in training at Wade's Mill. You shall come out with us—and if you like you can put the gloves on with him. The contest itself is a knuckle contest. And—a word in your ear.' He looked round and came close to Thurtell. 'It's fixed. Our man's the favourite. But he's going down in the tenth round. And that is as true and as sound as that Jack Thurtell has just lost two hundred guineas at billiards. I put you on to this by way of recompense. Do as you will about it. But you will be as safe as Carlton House in putting any amount on the other man, Carter. And you will get long odds. And now—good-day to you. Any time you would like a lesson in cue-play I am willing to give it.'

'I've had enough—from you.' Thurtell was half placated by being let-in on the cross, but still furious at having again set his own trap.

'Nay, I mean it. I mean a lesson. There are

several strokes I could teach you. And—who knows?—with a little practice of my method you might easily recuperate your losses from some of the sprigs and blades who attend here.'

'I shall remember. I thank you. Good-day to you.' Three paces from the doorway in Spring Gardens, he stopped, and his thoughts ran: 'Yes, I shall remember Mister God-damned Weare. And it won't be "Good-day to you." It'll be "Good-night to you." And your bag.'

On his way back to Haymarket, his temper cooled. Reviewing the occasion, he saw that he had accomplished one thing. Since he was set on punishing William Weare, he had now made it possible for himself to approach him without incurring suspicion or being rebuffed. He had paid a high price for it, but this price he might recover on the cross-match, and was determined eventually to recover by some means from Weare himself. Weare's friendliness, he could see, was false; he was just wide enough for that. He assumed it to be based on a hope that Thurtell's circle might let Weare into something good.

But just as Thurtell was in almost all matters a flat, so, on this occasion, was Weare. It was by that very attitude of assumed friendliness to Thurtell that he made possible his own violent end. Without it, Thurtell could not have approached him and invited him to the country.

·   ·   ·   ·   ·

Within a fortnight of their meeting, Thurtell was in funds. Weare's advice proved sound. Their man, the hot favourite, went down in the tenth round, and by a series of bets placed with different legs, Thurtell netted six hundred pounds.

But six hundred pounds does not balance many weeks of West End life. The Cock had become the resort of jockeys, bruisers, trainers, black-legs, and their hangers-on; and entertaining these people, or, which was worse, being entertained by them, was costly. In success or failure, Thurtell was always fated to be the apparent leader and the actual outsider, and his management of The Cock was another proof of this.

The arrival at The Cock of himself and his brother Tom had not improved the tone of

Haymarket—loud as it then was. The nightly rowdyism at their house had made 'The Thurtells' a by-word. Neighbours said they would be glad when the street was rid of them; some of these neighbours kept discreet brothels, and disliked the blunt attitude to things which was the style of the Thurtells. A few of the well-informed hinted that the neighbours wouldn't have to wait very long. Things were moving against the Thurtells from more than one direction.

Only at week-ends was The Cock comparatively quiet, for at week-ends Thurtell was not there. He was with friend Probert.

Probert, a wine and spirit dealer, and an ex-convict, had a snug little retreat at Elstree. He had rented it furnished, with shooting rights. It was at this Gill's Hill cottage that Thurtell spent his Sundays. It made a pleasant country lodging for him, and it was so remote a place, and so secure, that it was useful to know. One could lie low there, when one required to lie low, and be as safe from bailiffs as in the King's Bench itself. Probert had found it a very useful base; so useful, and so unknown, even in its own district, that he had established there a jigger, or secret still. For some time he and a friend had drawn two hundred pounds a week from the jigger's work, until some officious person of the district did learn that there was a cottage at Gill's Hill, and two excise men were seen in the local Elstree tavern. This compelled them to break it up; and the loss of this income, added to gambling losses, made Probert always ready to listen to any schemes put forward by the group in Haymarket. He clung to Thurtell as a flat who might at any time be a source of money, or at any rate of the means of money. And he made Thurtell a frequent visitor to the cottage.

The company of the cottage, other than himself, was his wife (a sister of his friend Noyes); her sister, Caroline Noyes; a maid; and a house-and-stable boy. One of the attractions of the cottage for Thurtell, besides the shooting and the privacy, was Caroline Noyes. The dashing Fanny had been quietly dropped, some time ago, in an odd corner of that continent of darkness between Clare Market and St. Giles's Rookery. She wasn't likely to find him or to trouble him again. He was now set on Caroline Noyes, who, added to what was called her 'agreeable person,' had useful expectations from an uncle.

But Caroline Noyes was already half pledged to another friend of Probert's—the man Wood; and the man Wood was down in Thurtell's book with the man Weare. Wood's appearance at The Cock meant always a scowl on Thurtell's face and flashes of temper against the waiters and the servants.

.   .   .   .   .

About September of 1823 they were sitting in an upstairs room of The Cock—Thurtell, Probert, and Hunt—drinking, and reviewing their situations. None of them was in good state. Each of them was slipping down, and was aware that he was slipping. Probert was being pressed for rent of the cottage, and hadn't got it. Hunt's engagements were falling off, and, since his association with Thurtell, he had been dropped by his rook-friends, Lemon, Cox, and Weare. And Thurtell was being pressed by creditors of The Cock; was being pursued by the Fire

Insurance Company; and was in danger of proceedings for fraudulent bankruptcy in Norwich.

Into the windows of The Cock, which stood
about where the Carlton Picture Theatre now
stands, poured all the harsh notes of the London
of the eighteen-twenties. Iron wheels and hoofs
on cobbles. The lashing of whips. The bawling
of coachmen and draymen. The yelling of
acquaintances greeting each other. And, threading
through them, the cries and songs of hawkers—
the lavender woman; the chairs-to-mend man;
the Newgate Ballad man; the knives-to-grind
man; the fish-hawker; and the milk-below
woman. Blind and sore beggars were wailing
for alms. Street musicians, with Pan-pipes,
trumpet and drum, were making din near the
Italian Opera. At the entrance to St. James's
Market a fight was beginning between a groom
and a dog-stealer; a group of dandies were watching it, and laying on one or the other. Outside
Fribourg's snuff and tobacco shop Crockford was
talking to Lord Windalong. Just at the door of
The Cock, Pierce Egan was engaged with Robert
Cruikshank. On the other side, William Weare

was coming up from his morning visit to Rexworthy's. Bishop and Ruthven, the chief and
second of Bow Street, were quietly promenading
and keeping eyes open. As they passed The
Cock they gave it a look;—one of those com-
prehensive looks.

.   .   .   .   .

Thurtell helped himself from the brandy bottle.
In company he was generally silent, but sometimes
he would break his silence with fluent obser-
vations, or with a rush of raging profanity. On
this occasion, after staring some minutes at his
glass, his silence flared into rage. 'So Wood's
fixed himself with Caroline, has he? Hope he
gets her, don't I? Damn his eyes—either he
gets out of my way or he's put out.' He glared
at Hunt and Probert. His face was dark-flushed.
'Wood better be told that.'

Probert said: 'I'll see he is. Don't like the
fellow meself. Nobody I'd rather see get the
girl than you, Jack.'

'Urr. Wouldn't take me long to deal with
Mister Wood. I've got a stick. A stick I had

73

sent down from Norwich. Prime little stick. An air-gun. A taste of that would settle Mister Wood. And settle another, too—one that got three hundred pounds of me. And settle Mister Barber Beaumont, too. One of these nights you'll hear of an accident in the Park.'

'Who's Barber Beaumont?'

'Beaumont, rot him, is director of the Fire Office. The one who's making all this fuss about our fire. And who put him on to it, d'ye think?'

'Couldn't guess.'

'That God-damn Fanny of mine. I shook her over a year ago. Shook her to rights, I thought. At the Oyster Saloon in Brydges Street, by Covent Garden. You know the place. Nothing to do with oysters, of course. She was lushy, and I saw the old Madam had her eye on her for a nice addition to her seminary. So I shook her on to Madam. I thought it had worked. I've never seen her since. But I hear now that she stored it up for me, and it was her that went to the Fire Office and gave them the tip. Rot her!'

Probert drank and scowled. In those days it

was a man's world. His remark—'Rot all the women, I say '—met with general approval.

'Ay,' said Thurtell. 'Agreed. But meantime, where are we to find the blunt, the ready?'

'Ay, where? Any ideas?'

Hunt, who had said little, spoke up. 'I know where there's fifty, if not more, to be made. But it's a tricky business.'

'What is it?'

'Why, some of the swell gaming-houses are forming a protection association. The Irish gang have been getting in. And when they lose, they smash the tables and the glass, and beat the attendants. And demand their money on threat of informing. I'm told that the owners would like to be rid of 'em. And would think fifty pounds a head cheap.'

Thurtell considered. 'Sounds like easy money. My little stick might be of good service. Air-guns do go off sometimes without warning.'

Hunt looked at him with a touch of admiration. 'You're a bang-up blade, Jack. Hard as steel.'

'Bah! What is there in life or death to be

afraid of? Nobody can shake me. Not even Jack Ketch. When things are tight, as devilish tight as they are now, nothing'll hold Jack Thurtell. Where can we find this protection association?'

'I heard them talking of it in St. James's Square. We could——'

The door swung open. The three men shot round in their chairs. In the doorway stood a heavy-jowled fellow in a long and dirty brown coat—one of Thurtell's hangers-on. He held up a hand. 'Sorry, gents. No need for alarm. But, Jack—there's warrants out for you and Tom. I got the tip from a Bow Street pal. Conspiracy to defraud.'

Thurtell got up. 'Thanks, Jim.' He turned to the others. 'Lads—I got to make a bolt somewhere. But where? Not your place, Probert. Too far out. I want somewhere in town, where I can keep an eye on things. Anybody know a safe hole?'

Probert said: 'I know a good man.'

'You do? In town?'

'Ay. Tetsall. Keeps the Coach and Horses

in Conduit Street. Knows all about keeping gemmen private from the bums.'

'Good. Can you introduce me there?'

'Any time. Do it now, if you like.'

'The sooner the better. Jim—call a coach. Then pack up and follow with my things to Conduit Street. The Coach and Horses. But get the coach first. In quick time. Hurry.'

He stood looking hard-eyed into the air. He was not now the bright blade who had arrived from Norwich. He was blunt and soiled and savage. The primary good in him had faded into grey ; its colour had been absorbed by his devil. Every move he now made was but another step to the appointed end, and his schoolboy hate of Weare was only setting the pace.

'Coach at the door, Jack.'

'I'm with you!'

VI

THE Coach and Horses in Conduit Street was a quiet, well-conducted house. But different as it was in this point from The Cock in Haymarket, its company was not markedly different. It was a place of accommodation for gentlemen who were wanted at the suit of John Doe and Richard Roe, and gentlemen of that sort had much in common with the Thurtell sort. There they could live concealed, and even if the tipstaffs traced them to the place, it held various devices by which they could always be ' out.'

With the addition of the two Thurtells and their visiting friends, Probert and Hunt, it became not so quiet. Any profit resulting from their stay must have been outweighed by the trouble they caused—a trouble that was to end in the landlord, a wholly innocent man, being seized by the redoubtable Bishop, and conveyed, as his prisoner, to the Watford magistrates.

On an evening of October, Thurtell was told that Mr. Hunt, the singer, was below, and desired to see him. He ordered him to be brought up, and Hunt came—not so dandiacal as he had been; indeed, definitely shabby and weather-worn. Thurtell was supping off a dish of chops, and invited Hunt to join. Hunt made no polite excuse. He pulled up a chair with eagerness, and fell to.

After clearing one chop he said to Thurtell, nodding towards the door: 'Are we all snug here? Anybody likely to overhear?'

'No. Nobody comes down this passage.'

'Good. I've a plan. . . . We're all broke for the ready. Well, why don't you take it ? '

'Where?'

'Weare.'

'Blast his eyes—what of him?'

'Well, he's got enough to set us all up. You know about his *bank*—the pouch he carries on him?'

'Of course. Thought about it a lot.'

'So have I. And I've seen the time when he was carrying seven and eight hundred on him. A great shame when poor fellows need a few flimsies. He won't put his money in a public bank. Always carries it. You owe him one, don't you? Well, I've thought of a way to settle that score and help ourselves as well.'

'How?'

'Get him in the right place and—out him.'

'No chance. We'd never get him in any place where it was safe. I've had my eye on him ever since the Shire Lane night. But he's a cunning reptile. He gives no chances. I followed him one night for two hours round Drury Lane and Holy Land, and never got a chance.'

'There's one place where it could be done safe.'

'Where?'

Hunt leaned across the table and whispered—'*Elstree.*'

Thurtell opened his eyes. ''M . . . Probert's place. Yes, good place. But no possible hope of getting him there.'

'That's my plan. Now, you're on fairly friendly terms with him, ain't you—so far as he sees? Well, invite him down for a day or two's sport at a friend's country place. Partridge shooting. And tell him—*tell him*—that you're taking down a young man, a Captain What-Not, who's just come into considerable property, and likes a flutter. Tell him there'll be back-gammon—he's got a rigged board for that—and blind hookey, and French hazard. And that the pigeon plays high and is worth plucking. Put it to him as a business matter—that you'll want a share for the introduction. That he must finance you in return for meeting the man, and that you'll repay him a percentage of what you win—to go on top of his own winnings from the bird. Then he won't suspect. And it should make him bring a good-size bank with him.'

Thurtell pushed the bottle towards Hunt, and frowned. 'Gard, I believe it's a pretty idea. I believe he'd bite. He still thinks I'm flat. But where shall we do it? At Probert's place?'

'No. On the way there. I haven't been there, but it's all quiet country round about there, ain't it? There must be lots of quiet spots—copses or glades.'

'Yes. Now I think of it, there's some very suitable lanes and hollows for such a job. Yes, and all round Elstree there's lots of useful ponds—marshy ponds. Which would hold anything put into 'em, and hold 'em fast. Yes—it's an idea. We'll have to have Probert in it, I s'pose, as we shall be on his ground.'

'Yes, but we needn't have him in too deep. Just say you want to work something on the way to his place. And if he keeps his mag close he can be in it without risk.'

'Yes, that'd be all right. He'll have to know something about it; otherwise, if something went wrong with the works, he might let things out without knowing he was letting anything out.'

'Perhaps you're right. If we did anything near his place, and didn't let him in, he might let things out anyway. He might actually blab. I wouldn't trust that——two yards. . . . Well then, when shall we try it?'

'The sooner the better. Let's see—this is Tuesday. What d'you say to the end of the week?'

'Excellent. Probert always goes home on a

Friday, and that would help the thing out. We could go down in two parties. Me and Probert. And you and Bill Weare. Probert could drop me at the spot you fix on. And I could hide there and be ready when you come along, to help you—if you need help.' Hunt didn't put great spirit into this last remark.

Thurtell got up and paced the room. 'You're a man of ideas, Joe. If you only had a bit of pluck you could be at the top of things in the flash world. . . . Well then, I'll see Weare to-morrow. And do you see Probert and tell him as much as he need be told. I shall want a pair of pistols. I haven't used any since being in town. I saw some at Bow's, in Marylebone High Street. I'll give you the money. You can get them for me to-morrow.'

'I'll do so. And don't forget not to let Probert know too much. He needn't know his name. He's never met him, and he needn't. The less he knows, the better. Weare'll just disappear from Lyon's Inn and the Brown Bear; and that'll be all. Nobody'll know anything but us two.'

'Very well. Come and see me to-morrow night. I shall know then whether we can get him, and what the arrangements are. If it's all right, we can fix the rest of the details then. Meantime, I'll send him a note at Rexworthy's.'

.　　.　　.　　.　　.

To Mr. William Weare, making his usual morning call at Rexworthy's, on the look-out for flats, the page-boy handed a note. It was a friendly note signed J. Thurtell. It offered Mr. Weare a few days' shooting at Elstree (Thurtell had chuckled as he wrote the 'shooting'); and after bagging a few birds there would be a handsome human one to pluck—a young man of good estate who had just reached his majority, and who liked to play high. If Mr. Weare could finance the play (for self and Thurtell) there should be goodly pickings for both. If Mr. Weare was agreeable, perhaps he would send word to Mr. Thurtell by the bearer. Mr. Thurtell proposed, subject to Mr. Weare's approval, Friday evening. Mr. Thurtell would await him in his gig at Tyburn Turnpike (another chuckle) at half-past five.

.   .   .   .   .

Weare smelt only gain, and on Friday mid-day, October 24, 1823, in his chambers at Lyon's Inn, he ordered his servant to get him a chop and potatoes, for three o'clock. He then began to pack.

Into his carpet-bag he put first his backgammon board and dice. Then a shooting jacket and leggings, Wellington boots, breeches, shirts, socks, stockings—all the material for a short and informal country visit. Then he cleaned his double-barrelled sporting gun and put it in its case.

He had mercifully no knowledge that within five days all these things would be in the possession of the police, and on public view at Watford.

At three o'clock he had finished packing his bag—for the last time; and by half-past three he had eaten his last meal. At four o'clock he put on his buff waistcoat, his olive-coloured great-coat, and his black castor, and gave his servant

85

the last directions he was ever to give. He said he was going out of town, and would be back Tuesday midday. He asked for a hackney coach.

The maid went out to the Strand, and had a ride in the coach up Holywell Street. Outside the door of his chambers she helped to put the gun and the carpet-bag into the coach. She heard Mr. Weare tell the driver to go first to Maddox Street, where he wished to make a call; and then to Quebec Street by Tyburn Turnpike. The coach then went off, and she saw no more of Mr. Weare.

.   .   .   .   .

While Mr. Weare was eating his last chop and potatoes in Lyon's Inn, Thurtell, Hunt and Probert were dining at the Coach and Horses. Considering they were all broke, they dined well on cutlets, a fowl, and brandy.

Thurtell ate in a businesslike way. His whole manner was businesslike. He dominated the table. Thurtell—fiery, brutal and bold; Hunt—quick, unscrupulous, but timorous; Probert—

heavy, slow, and cunning. Yet of these three, the dominant was to suffer, and the ineffectual were to wriggle out.

He turned to Hunt. 'Well then, it's all fixed. I've got him for half-past five. He snapped at the bait like a starved fish. You've seen to everything—the sack, the rope?'

'Yes. They're in Probert's chaise.'

'Very well. Probert, you'll take Hunt down in your chaise. I bring my good friend in my gig. I'll have to start a bit before you, as I've got to pick up the friend, and I've got a gammy horse. You'll overtake me quite quickly. And Probert—I want you to see that Hunt gets out at Phillimore's Lodge. He doesn't know where it is, so we must leave that to you. That's all that need concern you in the matter. You can leave the rest to Hunt and me.'

Hunt asked: 'What time d'ye expect to be at Phillimore's Lodge?'

'About eight, I should say. You should be there well before that, with your fast mare. If I'm late, wait for me. . . . And now, as it's getting on for five, I ought to be off. But as we've got some real work before us, we'll have some punch to keep our strength up. Ring the bell, Joe.'

The punch was ordered, and within ten minutes a bowl was brought. Thurtell filled the glasses, and when the waiter was out of ear-shot, he looked at the others. He was in pleasant mood, but his look was still a glare. 'Well, lads, if all goes well to-night, we should be pretty flush to-morrow.'

'Ay, and need be,' Probert growled. 'I'm about at the end of things. If something don't happen soon, I shall have to take a quick farewell of Elstree. Who's your man?'

Thurtell set down his glass, and went to a coat rack and took down a red shawl and a box coat. 'Never you mind. You've never seen him, nor never will.' He put the red shawl round his shoulders, and then got into the coat. From a drawer he took the pair of pistols. 'You primed these pops, Joe?'

'Yes. They should do the business.'

'Good. Then go down and tell 'em to bring the gig round. You can finish the bowl while

I'm on the way. But don't sit lushing too long, because I want you there when I arrive.'

.   .   .   .   .

In another ten minutes he was in his black gig, bowling down Oxford Street. At a quarter to six Hunt and Probert were in their chaise, following his tracks.

Twilight had fallen, and the lamps in the road and in the shops were lit. The grey-and-rose effect of twilight and faint lamplight made a good surround for their departure; it was just the atmosphere for those who wished to escape observation.

None the less, they did not escape. Sharp eyes picked them out of the haze.

When Thurtell reached Quebec Street to take up his friend, a woman, standing in a doorway, saw the black gig, and then saw him. While he waited, she kept in the doorway to see what his business was. Within a minute or so she saw a coachman come down the street carrying a carpet-bag and followed by a short, bearded man carrying a gun-case. She saw these things put into the gig; she saw the bearded man climb into it; and she saw Thurtell turn the horse down Edgware Road.

She looked after it, and her thoughts were: 'My faithful Jack. Up to something shady, I'll be bound.'

She turned and walked slowly up Oxford Street; slowly enough to reach the middle at about six.

Probert, unworried by what was about to happen, was thinking of future appetite. 'We shall be wanting some supper when we get there. And as there'll be three of us there may not be enough in the house. I'll pull up at this butcher's. Do you slip in and get a loin of pork. Pork chops'll be good on a coldish night like this.'

So Hunt got down and went into the shop and bought a loin of pork. As he came out with the parcel he brushed against a sauntering woman. She looked after him. She saw him get into the chaise, and heard his companion say: 'Now we'll be after them in prime style.' And she saw the chaise go spanking down towards Tyburn.

'M. . . . And his precious crony Probert, too. Wonder what they're up to?'

She looked down the misty, twinkling road, and her eyes, which were naturally hard, went harder. 'I didn't mind you shaking me, Master Jack. I was sick of you, anyway. But to shake me in that place. . . . Well, you haven't shaken me yet, so don't you think it.'

She wandered on towards Holborn. When, on Tuesday, she heard of certain doings, she remembered what she had seen.

VII

FOUR MEN GO TO ELSTREE

THE four men went on to Elstree. Thurtell drove as rapidly as his horse allowed. He made but one stop—at Edgware, when Weare suggested a drink. Thurtell, knowing it would be the last, allowed him to have it.

The followers, having a fresh and spirited horse, made a pub-crawl of it. And thereby fixed themselves in many minds. They had not gone far down Edgware Road before Probert said 'Have you a mind to a wet ? I have. There's a good place just here. Harding's. I supply them with stuff.'

So they stopped at Harding's and had brandy-and-water. Probert then felt fit to continue the journey, and they went on. As they went through Kilburn, Hunt gave Probert a nudge. 'There they are. There's Jack's gig. Just in front. Drive by and take no notice.'

Probert said: 'We've caught 'em up quickly. In spite of that stop. His horse must be a broke 'un.'

'Yes. Pass 'em and keep on. Get well ahead. All's right now. Jack's got him.'

'Who is it with him?'

'You don't have to know. You never saw him. You know nothing of him.'

Probert touched the horse and they dashed ahead. Two miles from Edgware, on the London side, he said 'There's the Bald-faced Stag. A prime house. We're well ahead. Let's have a wet here.'

So they stopped at the Bald-faced Stag and had brandy-and-water. While they were drinking, Probert, looking through the uncurtained window, said: 'Rot it. There goes the gig.'

Hunt, whose zest for the affair had passed out with the planning of it, said 'That's all right. We've got a slap-up horse. We'll soon overtake them. Let's have t'other glass.'

They did. But despite their stay they could

not keep behind Thurtell. Probert, under the brandy, let the mare have her head, and before Edgware was reached, they again overtook and passed him. Hunt's hopes fell. But when, in Edgware itself, Probert pointed out 'Clerke's place, the White Lion, famous stuff they keep there,' his hopes rose. He demurred at Probert's suggestion of stopping. He pointed out that they must be at this place called Phillimore's Lodge by eight. Probert said they could be there well before eight, and still stop as often as they wished. And Hunt, having placated his conscience with a protest, gave in.

So they stopped at the White Lion, and had two brandies-and-water. While they were having the second, Probert went behind the bar to speak to the landlord. Hunt stood at the door. From that position he saw Thurtell's gig come up and pass. It was going at a fair pace, and he was not sparing the rather sullen horse. Hunt stepped back, and watched it out of sight. A minute or so after it had vanished into the night Probert came out.

'Has he passed us?'

'Haven't seen him so far.'

'Good. Then we can have a little stop at The Artichoke. Nice place, The Artichoke. Jack and I have had many a lush there.'

'We'd better keep a look-out as we go,' Hunt said.

'By all means. I certainly thought he'd have passed us while we were in here. But we're bound to catch him at The Artichoke. He'll have to pass there. Even if he has slipped ahead without our seeing him, we'll overtake him before The Artichoke. Go on—up you get. I'm just in the mood to drive straight to hell.'

With a flick of the whip he started the horse, and the chaise went dashing out of Edgware towards Elstree. It went from one side of the road to the other. It seemed that Probert was anxious to advertise their presence on the Elstree road that night. The various halts, and his reckless driving, all fixed them in the memories of certain people who, unnoticed by themselves, were noticing *them*.

When they arrived, with snap and flourish, at The Artichoke, at Elstree, they had passed nothing like a gig, nor had anything like a gig passed them. 'Wonder where he's got to ?' Probert muttered. 'Can he possibly have passed us since we last saw him?'

'Almost impossible,' said Hunt. 'He'll be along soon, I reckon. Perhaps his horse has gone lame and he's having it tended. Anyhow, if we wait here, and stay outside, we shall see him, and can quickly catch him up.'

'Yes; he's got to pass here. And there's a by-road I can cut down to bring you to the place where he wants you, before he can get there. We'll stay in the chaise, and have our drinks here. Hi, there!'

A man came out from The Artichoke, and looked at the two dim figures in the chaise. 'Brandy-and-water,' said Probert. 'Two.' He slung the reins round the dash-board, and prepared for a quiet drink. 'Funny he's so late,' he murmured. 'He was going a good 'un when we passed him just before Edgware. Keep your ears open for wheels. Let's have another brandy.'

They sat in the chaise and had another brandy.

Ten minutes—twenty minutes—thirty minutes they sat in the chaise, clothed in damp darkness through which the chaise-lamps sent two tiny beams. Five brandies-and-water were brought out to them while they sat. Probert began to be full of grunts. 'Tip us a song, Joe,' he said.

'Don't be so damned foolish,' Hunt said. 'This is no time for singing. How long d'ye think we ought to wait?'

'Oh, he's bound to come up soon. Let's have another brandy.'

'You don't think we ought to go on to that place?'

'Not until he passes us.'

Hunt did not press his point. They had another brandy, and Probert turned his head to the darkness behind them and listened. Hunt didn't listen. He knew there was nothing to listen for.

But though neither Probert nor Hunt heard the wheels of any gig, other people did. On that dark October night, between eight and nine, many people in the little hamlet of Elstree heard the wheels of a gig and the galloping of hoofs. Jimmy Addis, Probert's house-boy, heard them.

He heard them approach the Gill's Hill cottage, and he ran to the door, thinking to receive his master. There was no other house in that lane, and he was therefore surprised to hear the wheels go tearing past the cottage.

Many villagers heard them. In those days, farm-labourers who had to be up at four in the morning, and were frugal with fire and light, went early to bed. Many of them were in bed before nine o'clock, and many a night-capped head was thrust from the bed-clothes at the sound of those reckless, racketting wheels.

When that sound had been folded into the night, they heard more wheels. For an hour of that October night, the silent lanes of Elstree were racked with the sound of horses and of wheels. In one of the vehicles were two men who had a rendezvous with death—one in an hour's time, the other in three months' time. Two sporting blades in a black gig; a half-tipsy wine-merchant and a silent singer in the chaise. Four precious rips dashing about the Elstree night; none of them a welcome visitor at any respectable house, and none of them desirable to

98

the Elstree residents. The lamps of their vehicles threw fitful lights on the hedges and sandy lanes of that country; but they threw no light on their business. Hoofs and wheels—hoofs and wheels—and nothing to be seen but the bobbing of lamps. The sleepy cottagers said 'The flash London friends of that man Probert, no doubt. Having a flare-up to-night,' and tried to go to sleep.

But the hoofs and wheels went on—up and down. And after an interval of quiet, more hoofs and wheels; and then a halt, and the sound of somebody getting down. And then more hoofs and wheels. And then—in another part—outside Elstree—a shot—a cry—feet slithering on gravel—a babbling of words—a groan. And then hoofs and wheels going rapidly away; and later, hoofs and wheels going more slowly.

And then silence. No more hoofs; no more gigs; no more shots or cries.

But later—long past midnight—the villagers awoke again. Those who had time-pieces saw that it was two o'clock. Feet, this time—and murmuring—and dragging—and stumbling.

.　　.　　.　　.　　.

Outside The Artichoke the two men in the chaise looked at each other. 'No good sitting here,' Probert said. 'He must have gone on somehow—or something's gone wrong. Yet we've been on the road all the time.'

Hunt said: 'Yes; perhaps we'd better get on to that place, though.'

Probert said 'All right,' and unhitched the reins. The amount of brandy he had taken had no power now to fire him, and they went off at a trot. Hunt released a long sigh. It was certain to be over now.

When they reached Phillimore's Lodge, Probert pulled up; listened; and gave a hissing signal. No response. 'He's not here,' he said. 'Still, you'd better get down and wait, as he said. I'll go on to the cottage, and see if anything's happened there.'

Hunt got down and stepped into a little grove. Probert drove off and left him in darkness and solitude. In darkness and solitude he stood for over an hour. The brandy, with the kindness of brandy, prevented his thinking.

·   ·   ·   ·   ·

Beyond Gill's Hill Cottage Thurtell drove his gig at headlong pace until it reached a hedged lane near Battler's Green.

From time to time Weare asked questions about the cottage and the shooting, and about the lamb they were going to fleece. Thurtell answered at random, knowing that nothing he said would be repeated, disproved, or brought against him. Mr. Weare's mag would very soon be voiceless.

Twice he drove past Phillimore's Lodge—at eight and at a quarter to nine. Knowing that Weare had not been here before, and would not notice the repetition in the darkness, he went over the same ground two or three times, in a circle. As he drove he skinned the darkness for a sight of Hunt or of the lights of Probert's chaise. He could see neither.

He was not aware, on this night-drive around Elstree, that he would later be seen as a satanic figure in a black gig. He was not aware that he was a Son of Cain, with Murder in His Heart; a thing to be shunned by all honest men. He was, in his own view, just a man who was going to get even with the dog at his side—to out it and take what it had. It was a reasonable thing to do, and not a thing to think twice about, or for men to get distressed about.

Once or twice on the drive he slowed down that he might listen for wheels. He grunted, thinking 'Where they got to, rot 'em.'

Weare said: 'What you grunting about? Why are you slowing?'

'Not sure of the road. There's a lane turns off here, leading to the cottage.'

'We passed a cottage about half an hour ago. A boy came out.'

'Yes. That wasn't it, though. That's the farmer's who's going to give us the shooting to-morrow.'

The horse went on at a mild trot. 'Hardly a pretty road, is it?' said Weare. 'On a night like this. Dark as pitch. Not a soul stirring. Not a light to be seen. Damme, what a place to cut a man's throat.'

Thurtell laughed. He thrust his hand into the deep pocket of his coat. 'Yes. If I didn't know you better, Weare, I shouldn't feel comfortable here with you. Just the place for removing a public nuisance—eh?'

Weare echoed the laugh. 'Wonder if the place has ever known any bloody deeds?'

Thurtell said: 'No. Not that I've heard of. But it's going to.' And with the 'going to' he took the pistol from his pocket, pressed it to Weare's neck, and shot him.

Weare fell from the gig with a slither and in a heap. In two seconds, under that physical impulse which makes a wounded man confident that he has not been wounded, he was up. He began to go down the lane in a staggering run. Thurtell jumped out and was after him. 'Come here, you son of a——. Come here, you robber. You blind hookey expert.'

'Jack! Jack! Spare me. . . . Any money you want. . . . All my money. . . . It's yours. Jack—don't. . . . Spare me!'

Then Thurtell was on him. They wrestled on their feet until Thurtell got in a blow with the pistol. Weare crumpled, and they went down in a fierce tussle. They growled and snarled half-bitten curses. Weare mixed pleas with his

103

curses. 'Jack! Anything you want. Don't—don't.'

'I'll shut your mag for you. Lie down—damn your soul. Lie down. Quiet, dog—quiet.'

A sudden spasmodic blow from Weare's leg thrust Thurtell aside. They rolled; and then Thurtell was underneath, and Weare, in a last and tremendous rush of strength, was hammering him. For a space he felt sure that the plan was to reverse itself, and that he was to be the night's victim. Then he remembered that Weare was wounded and could not hold out; and he fought on. But Weare had him by the throat, with knee on chest, and he felt that he was slowly choking. If Weare held out for a few seconds more, there would be an end of Thurtell. He fumbled feebly at his waist for his knife. He drew it.

Then, as Weare's face came closer to his with the pressure he was exerting, he made a slash. The grip on his throat relaxed and he made a second slash. A deep groan rushed from Weare. He collapsed in a sprawl and Thurtell pushed him off.

He got up, panting and muddy, and a little

104

sick. He looked down at the figure which now was still, save for a faint flicking of the fingers. Then he bent, and in automatic rage he smashed the butt of the pistol again and again on the uncovered head. His wounded vanity was avenged. Without speaking, he talked to himself. 'Urr—that'll stiffen your filching fingers.' This mute talk was his way of thinking. 'Damn you—what a job you gave me. But you're quiet now. Mr. William Weare won't play the flat no more.'

He took the body by the arm-pits and dragged it into the hedge. He ripped open the clothing. 'Aha—the little bank. That's mine. The others don't see that. Watch and chain—gold, too. A purse. I'll let 'em see that. Pocket-book— twenty pounds. I'll leave that and let 'em find it with me. And tell 'em he disappointed us in what he brought.'

He straightened himself and peered up and down the black lane, and listened. He heard nothing; no hoof, no wheel, no step which might convey the warning of prowling villagers. All done very neatly and single-handed, and no alarm raised. 'More work than I expected, though. Gard—I almost thought he'd got me before I pulled the knife. Never guessed Bill Weare was a tiger. But where in hell have Joe and Probert got to? If Joe were here we could put him in the pond and done with it.' He looked into the darkness again, and listened. No sound. No sound at all save the wind in the bare branches.

He went to the gig, climbed in, clucked the horse to a trot, and drove back down the lane to Probert's cottage. He had just reached the gate when he smacked his knee and swore. 'Gard— the knife and his hat. And the pistol. All there in the lane. Ah, well—no matter. They'll have to help me get the body to the pond anyhow. We'll look for 'em then.'

.　　.　　.　　.　　.

The boy Jimmy Addis, after the false alarm of the gig wheels which raced past, had retired to a chair by the kitchen fire, and gone half-way into sleep. He was awakened by a real alarm—a ring at the bell.

He opened the door and came face to face with

the tall, stern figure of Mr. Thurtell. The boy, like most boys in early teens, had quick eyes and quick observation. In the moment of seeing Mr. Thurtell in the light of the hall lamp and the gig lamps, he saw that Mr. Thurtell had come in a gig, but that Mr. Thurtell was breathless, and that Mr. Thurtell's boots were covered with mud. Where the lamps fell upon his coat, they showed a number of wet stains which a country boy would recognise.

Mr. Thurtell was harsh and blunt. 'Your master here?'

'No, sir.'

'Ah, well, he's expecting me. I must have passed him. He'll be here soon. Put my horse in the stable and give it a feed. And put the gig in. I'll walk down the lane and meet him.'

'Yes, sir. Er—Mr. Thurtell, sir—there's a lot of blood on your coat and breeches.'

Thurtell swung round. 'Eh? Whart! Blood! . . . Well, so there is. What of it? I started a hare on the way down and bagged it. Never seen blood on a sportsman's breeches before—eh?' He looked down the lane peering into the darkness.

'Shall I take the hare to the kitchen, sir?'

'Eh?' The reply was absent; his gaze was still fixed down the lane, and he was muttering.

'Shall I take the hare to the kitchen, sir?'

'Hare? What hare? Whart? . . . Oh, the *hare*. No. No. Get along and put my horse up. And if your master comes while I'm gone, tell him I'm out looking for him.'

The boy led horse and gig towards the stable, and Thurtell went trudging down the lane. Jimmy Addis, being a boy, had a good look inside the gig. Gentlemen sometimes dropped a coin or two on the floors of gigs and chaises. He saw a gun in a case, and a carpet-bag, and a backgammon board. He didn't see any hare, but he saw patches of blood on the cushions. He concluded that Mr. Thurtell had given the hare to some labourer. He also saw that the horse had been in a sweat, and had been allowed to cool off without being rubbed down. He took little notice of these things at the time. His master's friends got up to queer games. He went on with the job and wished it were bed-time.

As Thurtell was striding down the lane he heard the sound of wheels, and soon he came face to face with Probert alone in the chaise.

'What in hell's been holding you fellows? Where's Hunt?'

'Where you said you wanted him. By Phillimore's Lodge.'

'Blast you for a pair of ugly-mugged bunglers. Leave all the work to me, and then expect to share the blunt. He should have been there at eight, and he wasn't. You must have been dawdling all the way.'

'But we passed you, Jack, just outside Edgware. We passed you twice, but Edgware was the last time. And we waited at The Artichoke for you to come up, so that I could run Hunt on to Phillimore's. However did you manage to pass us? I'll swear you never passed us since Edgware. That's why we waited at The Artichoke.'

'What a pox d'ye want to hang at The Artichoke for? Why wait for me? When you passed me you should have gone on and left Hunt at Phillimore's. No matter how far ahead you were. Hunt should have been there at eight. He wasn't even there at nine. But no matter now. I've done the job down another lane.'

'You've done it?'

'Ay. And by Gard I never had so much of a business to kill a man in my life. I thought at one time he'd outed me. He had me down. Those pops were no more use than pea-shooters.'

'Who was the stiff 'un?'

'You don't know him; and he's done now. You'd better go back and find Hunt. I'll wait here. I shall want your help later—both of you.'

Probert turned the chaise and went down the lane. Thurtell paced back and forth in the dark. He felt ill at ease—unusual with him. The thing hadn't gone as it should have gone. Hunt had missed the rendezvous, and Weare had set him struggling for his life and covering himself in noticeable blood. It should have been done swiftly and the body dropped in a marsh—all over in five minutes. Phillimore's Lodge was quite near the ponds, and if the fool had been there on time. . . . Now they would have to make a special journey to carry the body to some safe place. He broke into a mumble of

Haymarket profanity.   Somewhere in the distance
a dog's bark broke the hush of the night.   Gard—
if that dog was snuffling round that hedge. . . .

Then he heard the wheels of Probert's chaise
and looked up.   Hunt got out with 'Why, Jack,
however did you get here?'

'Flew, of course, you mouldy fool.'

'How could you have passed us? We were
ahead of you and waited at The Artichoke,
and——'

'Damme, don't start that all over again. I've
had it out with Probert.   It don't matter now.
I've done the trick without you.   Why the devil
did you let Probert stop boozing at his cursed
public-houses?   When you knew what was to
be done.'

'I made sure you were behind or we wouldn't
have stopped.'

'Sure me eyebrow.   You were to be at Phillimore's Lodge at eight—no matter where I was.
You weren't there.   Let it go.   The thing's
done.'

'Anyway, you had all the tools with you.'

'Yes, and a cursed use they were.   God knows

what you primed 'em with. I had to cut his throat.'

Without thought, Hunt spoke from the unconscious. 'Thank God, then, I was out of it.'

'Yes, I'll bet you do. And wanted to be. The Artichoke was useful to you.'

'Jack—you surely don't think I——'

'Of course I do. Don't I know you? But come—let's get in and get a drop of brandy or something. Probert ought to have a drop of Good left over from his jigger. Gard knows I need something. I've had to fight for me life. And there's more to be done later. We've got to find a safe place for the body.'

Probert went on with the chaise at walking pace. Thurtell and Hunt followed on foot in silence. As they entered the garden, the boy was at the door. Probert got out by the stable and took the parcel of meat from the chaise. He gave it to the boy. 'Take that to the kitchen. Tell the maid to give us a dish of pork chops. In an hour. And give her what help you can. We can manage the horse ourselves.'

The boy went indoors, and the three of them

entered the stable. In the light of the chaise lamps Thurtell produced a gold watch and chain. 'I didn't have time to go over him. But I got this. And I got a purse.' He produced it and opened it, and showed three sovereigns and some silver. 'The watch should fetch about twenty pounds. And the gun—it looks from the case like one of Manton's—should be good for a tenner. We'll see what else he's got later. And now for Gard's sake, let's get a drink. Anything, Probert—anything you got, or I shall—I shall—topple over.' His face went grey, and he staggered. Probert led them to the lamp-lit parlour.

VIII

THREE MEN SUP AT ELSTREE

THEY went through the kitchen, where the pork chops were being prepared, and entered the parlour. Mrs. Probert and her sister, Caroline Noyes, were sitting up for them. If there was any wildness in their appearance, it passed unnoticed. Mrs. Probert was not accustomed to seeing her husband and his friends come home in any other state. But the presence of Hunt was unexpected.

'Ah, my dear Betsy,' said Probert, 'here's Jack Thurtell. And here's a friend you've often heard me speak of as a prime singer. This is Mr. Joe Hunt, the great singer from Vauxhall, and a great London swell. I hope he will entertain us after supper.'

Mrs. Probert and Hunt acknowledged the introduction with a little bow. Mrs. Probert noted Hunt's dress, and wondered whether the term 'great London swell' was a drunken joke, a new bit of London slang, or whether Hunt had prepared himself for a character-song in costume. Thurtell crossed to Caroline Noyes, and gave her the hand that had so lately used the knife.

Probert set out chairs, and said 'Bring us a bottle of something, dear, and glasses. We're all tired.'

Thurtell sagged into a chair and let his arms hang. His face was haggard, but despite his general exhaustion he was still the most vital of the company. The brandy was brought; and while William Weare was stiffening under the damp hedge, and the kitchen of Gill's Hill Cottage was gushing hints of a merry supper, the gentlemen drank to the ladies with finicky leering smiles.

After a couple of drinks Thurtell gave Probert a close look, and said: 'What about our getting out of the way while the ladies prepare the table?'

Probert got up. 'Yes, we may as well. We'll stroll as far as Nicholls's place, and see if it's all right about the shooting to-morrow.'

'Isn't it rather late?' Mrs. Probert said. 'It's after ten.'

'No. He's a late bird. Likes his little drop.'

They straggled out to the garden, and closed the door. When they were away from the windows Thurtell said: 'We shall want a lantern. And better take a candle, too.'

Probert answered: 'We'll get 'em in the stable.' While he prepared the lantern, and put some candles in his pocket, Thurtell got the sack and cord from the chaise. They went down the lane in a body.

Thurtell kept up a muttering commentary on the affair. 'Needn't have had all this bother if you'd been where I said at the right time. He'd have been swallowed by the mud now. I began to think you beggars weren't coming at all and had cried off.'

Hunt again apologised. 'We were sure you were behind, or we wouldn't have waited.'

Thurtell grunted, and led them across a ploughed field and up a lane. With only the bobbing light of the lantern to guide them, they had to peer and stumble their way. At last Thurtell said: 'It's the second turning off this lane, Bill. No it isn't. It's the first. Here it is. Just here.' Probert flashed the lantern, and they saw the body drawn into the hedge. 'Never mind that for the moment. Look for the knife and pistol first. And his hat.'

Thurtell and Hunt lit candles from the lantern and went to different points. Probert went a few yards up with the lantern, and prowled here and there, pushing into grass and wet twigs. Hunt went kicking along the roadway, bending close to the mud. Thurtell went to the opposite bank and ran his hand here and there.

After two or three minutes of this, he asked: 'Seen anything?'

'No—nothing,' said Hunt.

Probert got up. 'Better leave it till morning, lads. It'll be light at six. I'll come out early. It'll be better if I come, as you're strangers. The local people know me, and won't be surprised to see me prying about, as they would with you. I can bring the dogs and say I'm taking 'em for a run. Where did you say the thing was?'

'Through the hedge here. Think anybody'll see that lantern bobbing about?'

'No. Everybody's a-bed here.'

'What about Nicholls? You said he was a late bird.'

'That was just to put the missis off. And anyway he's over Letchmore Heath way. There's hills between.'

'This way, then.' Thurtell climbed over a low hedge and they gathered round the body. 'There he is—the scurvy rascal. Quiet enough now, ain't he? No stacking of the broads now, Hunt—eh? Put the lantern down.'

He bent over the body, and pretended to go through the pockets for the first time. Out came the pocket-book. He opened it. 'Three fivers. And some silver in the waistcoat. Let's get underneath the waistcoat.' He pulled the clothing about, and opened the shirt. Nothing there. No chain or anything. He turned and looked up at the others. 'He can't have been

wearing the bank. Can't feel anything here.
You feel, Hunt.'

'Not me, thanks.'

'Well, you—Probert.'

Probert bent down and ran his hands over the
body. 'Can't feel anything at all.'

'He can't have brought it then. But why not?
Wonder if he suspected a plant? Damme, I
thought he'd have cut up better than that.'

Probert looked glum. 'This is a bad turn-out,
Jack. Hardly worth working such a serious job for.'

'Can't be helped, my lad. There's the fivers—
and the sovereigns in the purse. And we'll
split up what the watch and gun bring. Now
then—where's the sack? We'll get him in that.
Then we'll wait till your place is quiet, and the
women a-bed, and we'll come and fetch him
and dump him in your pond.'

Probert, who had picked up the lantern,
dropped it. It gave a faint hiss, and they were
in darkness. 'Wot? *My pond?*'

'Where else, you fool? There's no other pond
here. It's all along of your boozing that he's in
these parts at all.'

'But Jack—think—it'd be the ruin of me. By God, you'll not do such a thing as that.'

Thurtell soothed him. 'It's all right, Bill. All right. It's only for to-night. I'll come down to-morrow night and take him off your place, and put him where you nor no one else will ever find him.'

'But think, Jack. In my pond. And the landlord's talking of seizing. Supposing they drained it just after we'd gone.'

'Shut your mag, you fool. D'ye want all Elstree to hear? I tell you, it'll be perfectly safe. Perfectly safe. It'll only be till to-morrow night.'

'But if anything should happen to you. If they came to-morrow——'

Thurtell became savage. 'They won't, you fool. For to-night you'll do as I tell you. I don't want to get you into trouble, and I won't. To-morrow night I'll clear the thing away. But to-night there's no safe place *but* your pond. You and Hunt got me into this mess, and you must see me out of it. And if you don't want to be served like Weare, you'll do as I say.'

Probert, who knew his Thurtell, sighed deeply and said 'Very well. Very well.'

Thurtell and Hunt worked the sack over the body, and Thurtell tied it round with the cord. 'He'll be snug there for an hour or so, I reckon. And now let's get back. They'll be waiting for us.'

They went back as they had come, peering and stumbling. In the lamplit parlour Probert affected the cheerful host. 'Come, lads, sit to table. Where's the bottle? We're ready, Betsy, when the maid is.'

At supper they made an agreeable party. Thurtell covered his surliness and talked brightly of the Corinthian world. He excused himself from taking food, on the plea of feeling a little over-done. Probert pushed the bottle to him. It was odd that the leader, the fearless and brass-bound Jack, was the one whose appetite failed him. Probert and Hunt enjoyed their chops, and ate with relish. Probert was so thick that no mere threat of danger, nothing short of its material presence, could move him. He had already known prison. Hunt was timorous, but his fears and forebodings did not react upon his appetite. He could always eat. Thurtell, for the first time in his reckless career, seemed to be at pause. Something in this affair had stilled him, and he watched the others with a slight touch of superiority.

He and his companions talked casually—if a little drunkenly—of the week's happenings in town, and who had seen whom, and the latest play or operetta, and what was being worn in the Park, and the latest Carlton House rumours— all the chit-chat that might interest the ladies. None of them could have guessed that that meal of pork chops, eaten at Gill's Hill Cottage, Elstree, and purchased in Oxford Street, would by the end of next week be known all over England. It was mercifully hidden from the two women that within a few days they would be carried, as prisoners, to Hertford. They ate their meal in the cheerfulness of quiet minds.

When the maid had cleared the table, grog glasses were brought out, and Probert produced rum, lemons, sugar and segars. He set about making the grog, and the parlour offered a pleasant domestic scene. The fire burning brightly. The kettle singing on the hob. Mr. Probert engaged with lemons and sugar. The dog snoozing on the rug. Two London gentlemen, Mr. John Thurtell and Mr. Joseph Hunt, at ease on the sofa. The lamp throwing a soft light on the whole circle. Anybody peeping in would have called it pleasant, and the ladies thought it was. True, the gentlemen were just a little tipsy, but at that time it was correct that gentlemen, after eleven o'clock, should be a little tipsy. It made no blot on the pleasant scene and the pleasant hour.

Each of the ladies took one small glass of grog with the gentlemen, and then Mrs. Probert, stout and forty, said: 'Pray, Mr. Hunt, may we not be favoured with a song? Mr. Probert has told me so much of your singing.'

Mr. Hunt simpered, and was only too happy to oblige. Compliments passed about 'the ladies' on one side and 'the celebrated vocalist' on the other; with apologies that the cottage, which was rented furnished, afforded no 'pianoforte.' Mr. Hunt, in his turn, apologised for possible

123

deficiency of voice, owing to the damp night and the long ride he had had in an open chaise. Then, full of pork, brandy, and rum, he got up and obliged.

His first number was:

> 'Twas down in Cupid's Garden,
> For pleasure I did go,
> To see the fairest flowers, etc.

Miss Caroline declared this sweetly pretty, and begged to be favoured again. Mr. Hunt gallantly asked whether she would name any special favourite, and she named 'When first I met thee, young and fair. . . .' After this the ladies smiled and petted him; and he responded with 'Where the bee sucks. . . .'

Probert, well forward in grog, asked: 'Can't you give us a comic?'

Hunt said he could, and with a nice taste, considering the circumstances of the evening, gave them:

> The night before Larry was stretched,
> The boys they all paid him a visit;
> And bit in their sacks too they fetched,
> They sweated their duds till they riz it.

For Larry was always the lad,
  When a friend was condemned to the squeezer,
And he'd fence all the foss that he had
  To help a poor friend to a sneezer.

                    With a fol-de-rol . . . . . .

Thurtell scowled a little at this, and said he preferred something smoother. He asked for 'Here's to the Maiden . . .' or 'The Minstrel Boy.'

When the recital was done he brought from his pocket the gold chain of Weare's watch. He looked at it for some moments, and then, in a sort of drunken generosity, he got up and went to Mrs. Probert. 'Here, Mrs. Probert, is a chain which was given to me some time ago by a dear friend. But it seems to me more suitable for a lady than a gentleman. Pray accept it, I beg.'

'Oh, Mr. Thurtell. Indeed, such a lovely chain—I couldn't think of it.'

'But please. . . . Let me but fasten it round your neck, and you will see how it becomes you.'

'Oh, but really, Mr. Thurtell. . . . You are all kindness, I know, but it is far too fine a chain for such as I. Truly, I mustn't let you——'

'Come, Betsy,' Probert said, 'seeing Jack's offered it to you it's only good manners to accept.'

'Well, if that is how it is, then I will. Though I hardly like——'

'Put it on, and say no more about it, I beg,' said Thurtell. 'It was almost made for you.'

She put it on, and simpered and preened herself. Miss Caroline watched the presentation and did not seem too pleased. Thurtell seemed queer to-night; not merely in liquor but queer in manner.

'Now where will you gentlemen sleep?' said Mrs. Probert. 'If Caroline and I have the maid's bed, we can make her up something for the night, and you can have the big room and——'

'No, no,' said Thurtell. 'We wouldn't hear of it. We had no intention of inconveniencing you. We came down without warning, so we'll camp here. Just as we are. Pray don't disturb yourself about us.'

Mrs. Probert gave a wise smile. 'Ah, well, I suppose you'll make a night of it. I don't know what time it can be.'

Thurtell looked at his gold watch, which lacked a chain, and said 'Half-past twelve.'

'Indeed! As late as that. Then if you're sure you won't have the room——'

'Quite sure, Mrs. Probert.'

'Then I think Carrie and I will retire. Bill, I suppose, won't be following yet.'

'No, he's going to spend an hour with us.'

'Yes; bring us another bottle of rum, my dear, and some fresh glasses. Then we shall be all ship-shape.'

'It's going to be a bout, I fancy.'

Thurtell gave a large yawn. 'Yes; you can expect to see your Billy come to bed drunk enough to-night. Hunt and I will see it out on the sofa. Good-night to you, ladies.'

The ladies withdrew, with nods, and smiles, and finger-shakings at these 'sad dogs.'

Probert opened the second bottle of rum. 'They'll soon be asleep,' he said. 'Then you can finish your job, Jack.'

IX

MRS. PROBERT LOOKS AND LISTENS

PROBERT was too confident in his statement. Miss Noyes, being young, certainly was soon asleep, but Mrs. Probert wasn't. At forty, pork chops and grog, at eleven o'clock at night, do not induce sleep.

Mrs. Probert lay awake, and turned from side to side.

She did this for some half-hour. Then she stopped turning and got up. She was aware that during that half-hour she had been muzzily hearing things. Now that she set herself to hear, she found that things were going on downstairs. Things that were not a usual part of a bottle orgy. She had always been a little suspicious of the queer fish her husband picked up in London, and she had never liked that man Thurtell, pleasant as he always was. She had her doubts about that gold chain. And she had her doubts about that shabby fellow, Hunt, though certainly his singing was all that her husband had said of it.

She got up and went to the door and opened it by a stealthy inch. She heard them at the cottage door. They seemed to be going out.

She went to the window. Looking into a dark garden from a dark room she could see with tolerable ease. She saw the three of them go to the stable, and then she heard the horse brought out.

She saw two of them lead the horse away by the bridle. She returned to the bed and took a coverlet, and put it round her shoulders, and sat at the window and waited.

Time in darkness seems longer than in light, and she felt that she had waited an hour before she heard them returning, slowly and with careful steps. She could see the horse led in, and she could see two dim figures; but she could see nothing clearly enough to identify which figure was which. Then she saw three figures round the horse.

She heard footsteps and a sound of dragging;

K   129

then round the corner of the house came three figures carrying something heavy. They carried this thing towards the carp pond, which, from her window, she could not see. But she guessed that they had gone to the carp pond, because next she heard a noise which she afterwards described as a noise like a load of fine gravel being dropped. Just the noise that a heavy thing would make when dropped into the middle of a pond.

She heard after that more footsteps, and mutterings, and other noises to which she could give no purpose. Then she heard returning steps, and saw the three dim figures re-enter the house.

When they were in, and the door shut and bolted, she left the window and went again to the door of her room. She heard a voice say: 'Now let's look over things.' And then the parlour door was shut. But she had seen and heard too much to seek a night's rest while her husband was still up. She pulled the coverlet more closely round her, and crept half-way down the stairs, till she was level with the key-hole of the parlour door.

There she crouched on the stairs, a grotesque

figure of Justice; a bulging woman of forty with dishevelled hair, robed in a patch-work coverlet. She listened. And she heard talk that revealed not only the doings of the night and the characters of those fellows Thurtell and Hunt, but also the character of the man with whom she had lived these many years, and of whose business and interests she knew so little. In those days wives were hardly expected to know what their husbands 'did.' They knew that their husbands went to London, and were engaged in 'business,' but few of them sought to know what that 'business' was, and when they did they were usually put off with vague abstractions. Many women then lived and died in complete ignorance of the nature of the work which kept up their houses and supplied their dress allowance.

This Friday night Mrs. Probert learnt a lot.

With all her nerves in her ears she first heard Thurtell's voice: 'There's a fiver each for us, and one of the sovereigns. Six pounds. That's your share of the blunt—both of you. The other things we'll split when we've realised on 'em. The purse and the reader we'd better burn.

Nothing in the reader except his gun licence and betting notes.'

She heard a rustling of papers; then a noise of ripping; and then heard something thrust into the fire and pushed down with the poker.

Then a voice: 'We'd better be off to town early—about four or five.'

'No. Too early. Attract remark. Make it eight or nine—a normal time. We must find the knife and pistol first. And I must sponge my coat. That cursed boy of yours noticed it. I left it in the stable. Get the bag and the gun, Joe. Let's have a look at 'em.'

She heard somebody go out and return. And then: 'It's locked. We'll cut it open.' She heard something cut open—the tearing of cloth— and then exclamations. 'His dice. Cogged, I'll bet. Yes, by God. Three packs of cards. Three.' She heard the noise of flipping through a pack of cards. 'Yes, of course. Look at 'em, lads. Real macer's cards. All chaunted. Gard, what an ugly brute. Ain't we served a good trick by clearing London of him? And the next to go'll be Wood. And then Barber Beaumont.'

132

Another voice said: 'This jacket fits me very well. I'll have this.'

'Take what you want. The gun's a good 'un. Manton's, as I thought.'

Then her husband's voice: 'I'll have one o' those packs. It'll be useful for a game at some of the places up and down the road. Better burn the others. And I'd like that yellow silk kerchief.'

'Have a care. It's marked.'

'I'll burn the mark out over the lamp. It's right on the corner—won't spoil the kerchief. Pass the bottle.'

She heard glasses filled. Then: 'You won't leave him there long?'

'No. On Sunday, Bill, we'll come down and clear you. Must go back to town to-morrow to take the things away. I'll bring a spade down.'

'If you're coming Sunday you might bring a joint down for the dinner. Beef, I think. Tetsall would get it for you. He has prime cuts.'

'Leave it to us. I'm going to clean my coat.'

'And I'd better get off to bed, or the missis'll be wondering what we're up to. What's o'clock?'

'Just on two.'

'Then good-night, lads. You'll be all snug here?'

'Yes. We'll make the best of it.'

'I'll be down early, and go out and look for those things. You'd better not be seen so early.'

She heard her husband's step moving to the door. Still keeping her crouch she turned and fled up the stairs to her bed.

The gold chain lay on her dressing-table where she had tossed it. Though she suspected it, she could not perceive its portent. There it lay : a vehicle of sore trouble to come to her whose neck had worn it, and of a rope to come to the neck of him whose foolish generosity had created an evidence.

X

TWO MEN FLY FROM ELSTREE

ON Saturday Hunt and Thurtell were off by ten o'clock, and had a busy day in town.

And on Saturday certain people had a busy day in Elstree. The landlord of The Artichoke was specially busy. People had to go somewhere to hear the latest and to talk it over; and The Artichoke was the most convenient resort.

Two labourers, turning in for their elevenses, brought the first real news. The place was full of rumours, but of real news there had been none until they came. The gossip had been of the noises that had disturbed the quiet of last night. Some had heard cries and groans. Some had heard a shot. Some had heard both. All had heard much scampering of hoofs and wheels.

All were convinced that something 'rum' had been going on last night.

The two labourers brought confirmation. After listening to the gossip, and taking a long drink, they looked at each other and nodded. One said 'Ar—they dunno all'; and began to tell his story.

At six o'clock that morning they had been working at the lower part of the lane, and farther up they had seen a stout man, whom they knew by sight, 'grabbling' in the hedge. He had a dog with him. When he saw that he was observed he went slowly off, looking back occasionally at the hedge. Thinking that something might have been lost, and that finding it might bring a pint or two of heavy-wet, they went along the hedge, one on each side, looking here and there. And what did they find?

With a sense for dramatic effect, they took long, slow pulls at their mugs, and then set their mugs down, and then looked blandly into the air with closed lips. One of the younger of the company said: 'Well—what?'

The spokesman of the two labourers said:

'Ar. . . I'll tell 'ee.' And didn't. Instead, he took another long, slow pull, and looked wise. When he had the company fully aroused, he said: 'Well, 'twere like this. We went scrabbling into hedge like, here and there. And there, sure enough, we found what it seemed this gent was looking for.' Another pause.

'An' what might that be?'

'Ay, what might it be? You may well ask that, Eli Emmett. I'll tell 'ee, not what it might be, but what it *were*.'

'Ay?'

'Ay. 'Twere a pistol.'

'A pistol?'

'Ay. We found a pistol. But that ain't all.'

'Noa?'

'Noa. Not by a long sight. It had new blood on it.'

'Blood?'

'Ay. Blood. And that ain't all.'

'Noa?'

'Noa. Fred 'ere found a knife. A bloody knife.'

'A bloody knife?'

'Ay. And that ain't all.' Another pause. 'Noa?'

'Noa. That ain't all. All about that part of the lane was mucky dabs o' blood.'

The company breathed an 'Arrr!' in chorus. And the younger man said: 'Then ther *must* a-been summin rum going on. I felt it in me skin. As I lay in bed I says to missis, I says—" Ther's summin rum going on out there to-night." That's what I said.'

'And well you may a-said it. There *were* summin rum. I ain't allowed to say too much for the present. But I know what I know. And you mark my words, Eli Emmett—ther's more going to be 'eard o' this. Ay, a lot more. And some people not far from 'ere's going to be sorry. Ay.'

'What ye going to do with knife and pistol?'

'We done it.'

'And what was it ye did?'

'I say no more. We done it—that's all. Ye'll hear more in a day or two.'

They stared at the speaker. Many years they had lived with him and had never realised his importance. Now he was enlarged and revealed as one apart from them. One who knew things. He was weighty with reserve; illuminated with impending drama. When he and his mate finished their pints and went out, the company said 'Good-morning ' with a note of respect which surprised themselves as they said it.

They fell to discussing the story, and then remembered a lot about last night which none of them had mentioned. Some of them had heard two shots. Some of them had seen dark figures wearing masks. Some of them remembered suspicious-looking bagmen who had been calling on shops in the village Friday morning. Some of them had seen a riderless horse careering through the night. One had heard a female voice cry 'Let me go, Sir Godfrey!'

The landlord, who knew his company, listened and smiled. He recalled the two men who had sat at his door in a chaise, and had taken ten brandies between them. Two men who more than once had audibly wondered where 'he' was. One of these men the landlord had seen before.

.   .   .   .   .

On the road to London Thurtell and Hunt made no stops for brandy. They stopped once only, to bait the horse, and arrived soon after midday. They drove first to Hunt's lodgings off Golden Square. It was Thurtell's proposal that Hunt should take charge of the 'things'—the gun, the board, the carpet-bag.

'You're all right. They can lie at your place and nobody'll think of looking for 'em there. It wouldn't do at my place, seeing they're after me on that conspiracy business. They might just happen in on me, and then search my place.'

Hunt agreed to the proposal and took the things in. When he returned to the gig, Thurtell handed him a packet of notes. He opened his eyes. 'What's this?' 'Hundred pounds there, Joe. Your share of the stuff. He did have a little bank on him. I found it when I did the job. I kept it quiet because I didn't reckon Probert was due for a share, hanging about on the road as he did.'

Hunt, with no qualms on the hanging-about, took his share joyfully. 'You're a swell cove, Jack, I must say. You do play straight. You could have kept this, and said nothing.'

Thurtell flushed under the compliment. 'I always do play straight with those who play straight with me. I never yet maced a pal. They say all sorts of things about me, but they can't say that.'

'No,' said Hunt, 'I've never heard that said.'

Back at the Coach and Horses he left Thurtell to see to the gig, and went loudly to the bar, and helped himself to another piece of the evidence which was to land him in Australia. In the bar he saw Thomas Thurtell, John's brother.

'Halloa, Tom.' He looked round the company, and called the attendant. 'George—a bottle of your best port, my lad. I'm going to drink wine now, and nothing else. Anybody want change for a fifty-pound note?'

Thomas Thurtell looked at his shabby and torn clothes and grinned. 'How d'you come by fifty pounds?'

'Oh, we Turpin lads can do it.' He brandished a bundle of notes.

Thomas Thurtell stared. 'Joe—whatever you been up to?'

'Bloody murder, of course; what d'ye think?'

Thomas Thurtell laughed, and the attendant laughed, and Tetsall, the landlord, laughed. Truth has that effect at times. Just then John Thurtell came down in clean, fresh clothes. Hunt hailed him. 'Come on, Jack. A bumper of port.'

Thurtell joined them. His brother, not quite at ease about Hunt's manner, took him aside; 'Jack—what've you and Joe been up to since yesterday?'

'Been out shooting.'

'Why—look at your hands—all scratched and torn. How d'ye get 'em like that?'

'Oh—ah—we've been netting partridges. In the brambles.'

'Where did Joe get all that money?'

'On the cross, I expect. You know he's got an eye for a pigeon.'

Thomas was satisfied and rejoined the party. Hunt was inclined to be in song, until Thurtell discouraged him. They and their wine were attracting attention in the bar. Thurtell overheard Tetsall the landlord remark on Hunt's clothes and general appearance to the attendant.

'I wonder a bang-up gentlemen like Mr. Thurtell cares to be seen with so seedy and shabby a fellow. And in a gig, too.'

After an hour's sitting Thurtell called him out of the bar. 'Come on, Joe. There's things to do.' Hunt obediently followed him out. He had always respected Thurtell for his cold, bold air. The voluntary handing-over of the hundred pounds had shown him not only bold but magnanimous.

'Now first, Joe, you must polish up a bit. You're making people notice you, and wonder. There's things in that bag at your lodgings. Fit yourself up with them. And there's some things of mine lying at a pawn-broker's in Fleet Street. Silk shirt, and a blue coat. Take this ticket down there, and get 'em out. Here's a fiver to cover the charges. I can't go myself, as I can't appear in those streets. I've got to keep snug. Take what you want from the bundle to rig yourself. And if I were you I'd get shaved. In fact, it wouldn't be a bad dodge, I think, to get all that beard off. Then if there's any trouble nobody who saw you Friday night would recognise you.'

'You're in the right, Jack. I think that's a good tip. I'll go home and do it now.'

'Do. And on the way get a spade. A good large spade. We'll take it down to-morrow. Probert's got nothing down there in that way. Don't come back here to-night or to-morrow. I'll pick you up in the morning at the corner of Golden Square. We shall start early. About nine.'

'Very well. Don't forget to order the beef, though, as Probert said. Or we shan't get a dinner.'

'I'll see to that.'

. . . . .

At nine o'clock on Sunday morning the black gig appeared in Golden Square, and Hunt was picked up. He was smartly dressed and in merry mood. Fears and apprehensions were gone. It was Thurtell the bold who was in abstracted mood. He looked Hunt over, and said casually: 'What a swell my Joe looks. Those things might have been made for you.'

'All aboard, me hearties. Have you got the

144

beef? Here's the spade.' He pitched it into the gig, and climbed in. Thurtell, without further word, touched the reins, and they went off again to Elstree. They were coming back from Elstree that night, and so far as their arrangements went that would end their connection with Elstree. Probert was giving up the cottage, and they would see it no more, and make no more journeys down the Edgware Road. Thurtell found that he had a keen distaste for the place. Not only had he no desire to see it again; he had a positive wish *not* to see it again.

But one more journey down that road they had to make. They were to make it on Wednesday in the company of Ruthven.

Just before they reached the cottage, and were going by the garden-wall, Hunt threw the spade over the wall into some bushes. 'Don't want them to see it in the house. We shall know where to find it.'

They were greeted by Probert with: 'Have ye brought the beef? I hope it's a good cut.' Nothing was said about the business they had come to do, or about the pond in the garden.

They passed the Sunday in the usual way of a country Sunday for their kind. Dinner, drinking, cards, tea. Not until late evening did they concern themselves with other matters. Then, while Hunt, by arrangement, was left to entertain the ladies and keep them within doors, Thurtell and Probert went out to take a walk. 'As far as Nicholls's place.'

Hunt did his best to entertain the ladies, but the ladies and the room gave him a feeling that he was not succeeding too well. His songs did not go as well as they had gone on Friday night. Now and then he caught Mrs. Probert, who was sitting away from the light of the lamp, with her eyes fixed on him. The third time the look was so prolonged after he had caught it, that, thinking she was going to speak, he said 'Yes?'

She started. 'Oh—er—I was thinking—I was thinking how smart you look to-night, Mr. Hunt.'

'Eh? Oh—ah—just my usual. I did look rather shabby on Friday, I believe. I'd—ah—been in the country some days last week, and came straight on here in my old togs. I hope I wasn't too disgraceful for your charming parlour.'

146

'Oh, by no means. In the country? I under-stood Mr. Probert to say he'd been dining with you each day last week.'

'Eh? Oh, no. Quite a mistake. You must have misunderstood him. I was at—ah—Croydon.'

'I quite thought that was what he said.'

'Then he must have been muddled. He does get muddled at times about people and things.'

'Yes, he does. . . . Those things fit you extremely well.'

'They should. They were made for me by one of the first tailors of St. James's. He serves the most elegant set.'

'Indeed. And that handsome black beard of yours. So romantic, I thought. What could have induced you to part with it?'

'Oh, well—I don't know how it is, but it became a trouble, y'know. And beards are no longer the Go at the best end of the town. A singer has to observe the fashion, you know.'

'Yes. Quite naturally.'

These remarks disturbed Mr. Hunt. He

wondered what she knew, or suspected, or whether they were the ramblings of a dull country wife. He was relieved when Thurtell and Probert came in. Neither had the appearance of having spent a pleasant two hours with Nicholls. They looked dark and downcast. But it seemed that things were now clear, and that they were free to break up; for Thurtell's first words were: 'Well, Bill, we'll just have a drop of your Good Stuff, and then I'll get the gig out.' He looked towards the ladies. 'It's been a pleasant Sunday, Mrs. Probert. Let's hope we'll have many more. If not here, then in another rural retreat.'

Mrs. Probert nodded in acknowledgment. Probert brought bottles and glasses. They drank standing. Thurtell took his drink hastily. 'Well, I'll get the gig.'

'But, Mr. Thurtell,' Mrs. Probert said, 'Jimmy can put the horse to the gig for you.'

'Thank you, Mrs. Probert, but I can do it twice as quick myself.' He went swiftly to the door while saying this, and looked at Probert.

'Are you in such a hurry, Mr. Thurtell?'

'Not hurry, Mrs. Probert. But I promised to

148

meet a man in town by midnight. And I don't want to force the horse.'

'Anyway,' Probert said, 'I want Jimmy myself. The cask's leaking in the cellar, and I want him to fit a new spigot.'

Thurtell got out, and in two minutes was back. They made farewells, and urged the ladies not to come to the hall and meet the damp night air. It was so treacherous. The ladies agreed that October mists were always bad for the chest, and they retired to the fire.

Probert closed the front door behind them and they crossed the garden. The horse was in the gig and the lamps lit. By their light Hunt noticed a long package on the front of the gig. 'Get in,' Thurtell said. 'Quick.' When Hunt had but just got his foot on the dash-plate, Thurtell turned the gig, and it shot through the gate and down the lane towards Elstree.

Just before they came into Elstree he turned into a narrow lane and took a detour round the village. 'Where are we going?' Hunt asked.

'Elstree Ponds. Safest place. Couldn't use the spade. Ground too hard after the frost.'

At the pace they were going they quickly reached the ponds, and Thurtell drove the gig up to the edge of the larger one. It was a moonless night, and the water was black oil. 'Listen! Hear anything?' They both listened, and heard nothing. He jumped down, and spoke in curt mutters. 'Come on and help.' Hunt got down, and with some trouble they lifted the long package from the front of the gig. 'Now—as far in as we can. Swing with me—and fling forward at three.' They raised the package from the ground and balanced it. 'Now—one—two—*three!*' At the 'three' the package sailed outward to the middle of the pond, and went in with a hollow plop.

Thurtell looked at the ripples. 'Ugh. With his weight, and the stones we put in, he'll have gone down. Down. Into the mud. Finish. Domino. And now—London. London for us all.'

They sprang into the gig, and, once they were away, Thurtell, who had been moody all day, seemed driven by a devil. The horse was fast enough, but he lashed it on with 'Grr-up, ye brute—grrr-up!' and the gig went off at a rocking gallop. Hunt had to hold on. 'Grrr-up, I say!' They went hurling through the night.

'Hi—Jack, you'll have us over. Have ye gone mad?'

'No, I ain't. The alarm's up.'

'*What!*' Hunt almost shot out of the gig with his own start.

'The alarm's up. Nicholls is moving in it. It's all up.'

'Never say that!'

'We've got to be spry, then. It's a poor chance, at best.' He spoke in jerks from the swaying of the gig. 'There was talk yesterday— about the shot—and the groans. They were heard. And they've found the knife—and the pistol—in the hedge. And blood all over—the lane. We must have been—all squiffy—Friday night—to be so—careless. Nicholls is going— to magistrates.'

'My God!'

'Well, you needn't—appear in it. Keep quiet —that's all—for you to do. And lie low. But above all—keep your mag—shut.'

'Where we for—now?'

'London.   Conduit Street.'

'Conduit Street!'   Another start.   'But—Jack
—not there.   If the—people—connect anything
with—Gill's   Hill—they'll—soon   learn   that—
Coach and Horses was—Probert's hang-out.   And
they'll send there.'

'No.   Nothing of the—sort.   Just what they—
won't do.   They know we're—wide boys, and—
they'll guess we'd—never be such—fools as to—
go to our—known place.   That's the—last place—
they'd—think of—looking.'   The gig scraped a
mile-stone, and rocked.   'Blast that—stone.   Yes,
Conduit Street for me.   For a—day or two—at
least.   And then perhaps—Bristol.'

So the black gig rocked on towards Conduit
Street.   And here, once again, as always, the
fly-flat was a shade too fly.

Gallop on, Mr. Thurtell.   Wreck the black
gig and yourself, if you will.   Better for you,
perhaps, if you did.   A quick end instead of a
long-drawn end over three months.   This is your
last gallop.   You have galloped through your
twenty-nine years, but this is your last lap.

The karma that made you what you are, and set you to lay up a new store of good or evil, has brought you to this harvest. You are galloping straight to where disaster awaits you, as you did when you galloped from Norwich to London. Only—this is the final disaster. Nothing to be retrieved from this. But you face it boldly. Brute and flat, you are bold enough to face the harvest of what you sowed. By Gard—Jack will face it.

So hell-for-leather, Jack. Aldenham—Edgware —Kilburn Priory—Maida Hill—and when you reach the top of the rise, by the Harrow Road— straight in front of you—the lights of the Turnpike of Tyburn.

Through the gate—into Oxford Street—up Oxford Street—and so into Bond Street and the effacing sea of traffic and the comfort of crowds.

But not wholly effacing. A wandering woman at the corner of Bond Street sees you coming up. She sees you turn into Bond Street and get tangled in its mass of carriages. 'My faithful Jack. In a vast hurry this time. Got the devil behind him, I should think.'

As he became fixed in the jam she turned and walked down Bond Street on the off-side, and kept the black gig in view. 'Follow him, I think. Ruthven may like to know where he's hiding.'

.   .   .   .   .

By George Ruthven, of Bow Street.

"As soon as Hunt and Probert were lodged in custody, I left in order to secure John Thurtell. I found him in bed at Mr. Tetsall's, at the sign of the Coach and Horses, Conduit Street, Hanover Square. I said:

'John, my boy, I want you.'

'What for, George?' said he.

I replied 'Never mind; I'll tell you presently.'

Thurtell had been anticipating various proceedings against him for setting his house on fire in the City, by Mr. Barber Beaumont, on behalf of the County Fire Office. It was highly probable that he suspected I wanted him on that charge. He prepared to accompany me. My horse and chaise were at the door. He got in and I handcuffed him to one side of the rail. I drove towards

154

Hertford. On the road nothing could be more chatty and free than the conversation on the part of Thurtell. If he did suspect where I was going to take him, he played an innocent part very well, and artfully pretended total ignorance. We had several glasses of grog on the road. When we arrived I drove up to the inn where Probert and Hunt were in charge of the local constables.

'Let us have some brandy and water, George,' said Thurtell, after he had shaken hands with his associates. I went out of the room to order it. 'Give us a song,' said Thurtell to Hunt; and Hunt, who was a beautiful singer, struck up: *Mary—list, awake!* I paused, with the door in my hand, and said to myself: 'Is it possible that these men are murderers?' "

XI

MR. THURTELL FACES THE MUSIC

THE music that John Thurtell was facing was engraved on the whitewashed walls of his cell in Hertford Gaol. A flat to the last, he had trusted his confederates; and the jackals had scuttered. That he was here was owing solely to them. Hunt and Probert had been taken. They had not been charged. They had been taken and asked if they knew anything of the events in Elstree of Friday night, October 24. They had hedged, and could have hedged. But just when the magistrates, being without a corpse to act upon, had been about to drop the case, Hunt, in fear of his life, had offered, in return for clemency, to show them where that corpse was. And Probert, in fear of *his* life (though he was to end on a scaffold elsewhere) had turned King's Evidence.

156

Those two were off. Probert, as Crown's witness, was acquitted of all and any charges; and Hunt, it was understood, would, if found guilty, be given the mercy of transportation. The fearless fly-flat was to be the only victim Justice would desire. He had dealt fair by all, and had come to this. They had played cross, and were to escape. Their karma had a balance. His had run out.

He knew what was coming. He was no dreamer or optimist. He saw a fact for what it was, and having no religion he did not pretend that bad was good, or might be good, or was to be tolerated as the best that could be. He saw it as it was—bad. And he knew what part he soon would have to play. It was a hard part, but he had always liked playing parts; and he would play this part with a straight back and a steady eye. He had lived as Dashing Jack Thurtell. He would die as Dashing Jack Thurtell.

The officer who was his constant companion in the cell during the day was surprised to hear a harsh laugh come from him. It was born of his thought: 'Weare went out in the dirty dark. It

157

fitted him. I shall go out in public in the daylight.'

There was no chance for him, he knew; none at all. The press had published him as the complete villain; had ferreted out all his little exploits which looked nothing when done, but looked something in print. And had ferreted out many that were not his. Already the public had accepted him as guilty of a dozen crimes. Already there were Seven Dials ballads about him; and a London theatre was even running a play based on the murder, with the black gig on view as one of the properties. Against the cloud of witness which the other side had prepared he was helpless.

He had heard from his counsel of their number— fifty-three in all. From this he had learned the truth that more people know Tom Fool than Tom Fool knows. Among the fifty-three were— Probert; Hunt; his brother Thomas; Mrs. Probert and gold chain; the host of The Artichoke; Tetsall of Conduit Street; Rexworthy, of the Billiards Room; Thomas Noyes; Caroline Noyes; Weare's brother; Weare's maid-servant; a police horseman of Edgware Road; the coachman who delivered Weare to him; the landlord of the White Lion; the Fleet Street pawn-broker; Jimmy Addis; Probert's maid-servant; the two labourers; Farmer Nicholls; three servants of The Cock; and Ruthven, whom he had found at his bedside with handcuffs.

He filled the cell with a long, deep sigh; then turned to the attending officer. 'Give me a pinch from your box, there's a good lad.' The officer passed his box and Thurtell took a large thumb-and-finger-ful. 'Ah—ah. A friend in need is a friend indeed. I have no friend now. I hope your friends, my lad, will never treat you as scurvily as mine have treated me.'

A key girded and ground in the great lock of the door. 'What's this—dinner?'

The Governor and a warder entered. 'A gentleman from the London newspapers desires to see you. You are at liberty to see him if you wish; or you may prefer to be alone. You have full choice.'

'Rot the London newspapers! See how they've baked me. Judged me before the case is heard. Prejudiced me so that a fair trial——'

'The gentleman gave the name of Mr. Pierce Egan, and said——'

'Pierce Egan! Pierce Egan to see me! Well, come, that's different.' Even at that hour his vanity was still assertive. 'I shall be honoured by a visit from the distinguished Pierce Egan— the pink of the Fancy. Pray, let him be brought in.' His face took a schoolboy flush.

'The rules do not permit that. He may not come here. But I can lead you to him. He waits in the office.'

'I will be obliged if you will take me there.'

Through various passages, which meant the unlocking of various doors, he was escorted to the office, a plain room with table and two or three wooden chairs. There he confronted a short, dark man. The man bowed. Thurtell bowed. He put forward his fettered hand in greeting. 'Pray excuse my iron gloves. It is indeed kind of Pierce Egan to make this visit.'

Egan smiled at the remnant of spirit. 'We have met before, I think.'

'Have we? I have long known Pierce Egan, naturally; but I did not know that we had met.

160

I trust it was in happier circumstances than those in which we now meet.'

'Once at Norwich, three years ago. And we exchanged a few words in London.'

'Did we indeed? I wish I could recall the occasion. Your face is somehow familiar. But that perhaps is because I have no doubt seen you in so many parts of the town. Where of course you would be—as the most celebrated chronicler of that world which was so lately mine.'

' I have of course observed you, Thurtell, in the Corinthian resorts. But—forgive me if I remind you of anything to distress you—we exchanged a few words at Kerrigan's—in Shire Lane. I took the liberty of giving you a warning.'

Thurtell brought his chained hands down on his knees. 'So *that* was Pierce Egan, was it? Gard, sir—had I but known, I would have listened. And well for me had I done so. Well, indeed. There, sir, was the beginning of my trouble. How often the small voice speaks and—I thought it was some pious simpleton. If only the name of Pierce Egan had been mentioned.'

'Say no more, Thurtell, I beg. I had no wish

to add to your present disturbances. You are looking well. Mighty well.'

'Why, yes, I do pretty well, despite my surroundings. I keep in good spirits.'

'That is excellent. That is the thing. With a good heart you will be better able to meet your accusers.'

'And I can. I assure you, Egan, I never committed any serious crime in my life. I never was before a magistrate. I have been a dupe, it is true, but an innocent dupe.'

'I sincerely hope you will be able to make a satisfactory and happy defence. One that will restore you to the world.'

'Egan—I will not impose upon *you*. I did not do that murder. I declare solemnly to my God I did not do it. One day—however it goes—all will come out.'

'I am content to hear you say so. And the two who were taken with you——'

'Egan—let it stop there. Never in my life have I rounded on those who have sat at my table. Nor, not at the last drop, will I. But I will say this—two such contemptible, cowardly rascals have seldom sat at my table. It's like being assaulted by one's own right hand. One doesn't know what to do. Probert and Hunt—a disgrace to mankind. And Probert by far the worse of the two. Hunt's timid, and can't help it. But Probert. . . . He's such a wretch that I can't keep my temper when I name him.'

'How are you faring here, Thurtell? Have you all you want? Are you out of money, or can I——'

'No, no. No. That's like your generous nature, and I thank you. But all's right in that matter. I am well found. But if I were not, that wretch Probert would not advance me a tester to keep me from starving. I know that. When we first arrived I lent him money to keep him from starving. And when I asked for a return of part of it, just after he had received five pounds, he sent me two shillings in a snuff-box. Think of that, Egan. And think what the story of such a man can be worth.'

'It sounds almost incredible. But I know the town, and I know a little of what apparently amiable men are capable of.'

'You do; and you should. Your wide experience and observation have given you every chance. And your works show it.'

'Well, I hope you will use your time well in preparing a defence. You know, I presume, what you have to answer?'

'Ay, I do. The cards are stacked against me now as they once were before. But never fear. I shall deal with 'em. They say outside it is a certain thing. But listen—do you suppose that I, the kind of fellow I am, would have passed so much time in this place if I had been guilty?'

Pierce Egan hesitated for an answer; and Thurtell went on: 'No, indeed I wouldn't. If I, Jack Thurtell, were guilty of that crime, I would have cut my throat ere now. Ay. I don't fear death. But the disgrace. The contempt. That is something. That, as an innocent man, I will fight. Let me read you something of my defence.'

'I would much like to hear it.'

Thurtell took a roll of paper from his pocket. Pierce Egan slipped his snuff-box from his waistcoat and offered it. 'Ah, thank you, my friend. That is something I am out of at the moment.'

'Then pray take the box. It holds half an ounce and was freshly filled this morning.'

'This is kind. I will be glad of it. And I will keep the box by me as a souvenir of Pierce Egan.'

.   .   .   .   .

Four weeks later Thurtell was still in Hertford Gaol. He was in a new cell, and he had as companions two warders instead of one.

He sat on his bed, elbows on knees, twiddling thumbs. 'Well, lads, that's how it goes. Now up, now down. Some lucky, some unlucky. The good 'uns suffering. The bad 'uns escaping it all. Some prosperous, some miserable—and neither doing much to bring 'em to it. You didn't hear my speech for my defence, did you?'

'No. We wasn't in court.'

'Do you hear how it went? Do you hear if it made an impression?'

'I did hear some people say they thought it wunnerful.'

'Indeed! That's gratifying. I put much trouble into it, I assure you.'

'I believe you.'

'I did. I am glad to hear it was remarked upon. It contained some striking passages, I thought.'

'So they said. But won't you compose yourself? Won't you lie down and take a sleep?'

'Sleep! Gard—I've time enough to sleep, ain't I? Let me look at the light. Let me look at the light. Let me look at those flowers the chaplain left. Let me look at your faces. In a few hours I shall have nothing to look at. Sleep! What does the great poet say—" We are such stuff as dreams are made on, and our little life is rounded with a sleep." '

Keys in the lock again. Two keys this time, and bolts. The governor entered. 'Are you comfortable, Thurtell?'

'As comfortable as man can be in my extremity.'

'Is there nothing I can provide to make this time easier? It is in my discretion to satisfy all reasonable wishes, and I will gladly exercise that discretion.'

166

'You are kind. But I think I want nothing. Stay—would it be permitted that my friend Hunt should spend the last night with me?'

The governor hesitated. 'Yes, I think that can be granted. I trust you, Thurtell, to behave decorously. You will understand my hesitation and my reason for asking.'

'I understand you perfectly. Believe me, I will behave as you yourself would behave. At this hour I bear him no ill-will.'

'I will bring him to you.'

The doors were locked and bolted. Two minutes later they were unlocked and unbolted.

Joseph Hunt came into the cell. Thurtell, still sitting on the bed, looked up at him and smiled. 'Well, Joe?'

Hunt, in his chains, looked sheepish and fearful. Thurtell got up and went to him. 'Joe, I've no one to thank for this situation but you. But I forgive you everything. As for your own case, you brought it all on yourself. But all's over now and all's forgiven. And Joe—I'd rather be where I am now than where Probert is—wherever he is.' Hunt had nothing to say. 'Come, cheer up, man. It's not so bad. You've still life before you—in another country. As for me—I'm prepared. I always was prepared. Sit down, man. You've done me wrong—and I think you know it—but that's all past. I've nothing to say now but—God bless you.'

Hunt sat down, and then broke down. He wept. Thurtell looked at him in gentle surprise. But he had always felt that Joe was not fitted for the flash life. Forgetting his own immediate condition, he set himself to comfort Joe. 'Brace up, man. Brace up.' Hunt was bowed over. His shoulders shook. 'I've done wrong. I've done wrong.' He moved his chained hands to Thurtell's chained hands, and gripped them. 'I've done wrong.'

'Well, well, it's all past now, Joe. You have years before you in which to repent. See that you use them well. Tell yourself it's for old Jack's sake.'

'I will, Jack; I will.'

'Won't you rest now, Mr. Thurtell?' one of the warders said. 'It's getting very late.'

Thurtell shook himself from side to side on

the bed. 'Rest! *Rest!*' The warder shrugged his shoulders, and gave an understanding nod. 'Tell me,' Thurtell went on, 'does the affair cause much noise in the town?' He was now, as always, anxious to know what effect he was creating. 'Is a large crowd expected to-morrow? Or rather to-day?'

'They say so. Every hotel and inn is full.'

'No doubt some are already waiting in the square?'

'They are, Mr. Thurtell. Hundreds of 'em.'

'Aha! I shall have a good send-off then. Plenty of sporting legs among 'em and flash boys, eh?'

'Yes, plenty o' *them*. The Mayor's a little disturbed. There's a thing that might interest you, Mr. Thurtell, if——. I'm not sure that I should mention it, but I suppose it can do no harm, and it might interest you.'

'What is it?'

'Why, they're keeping fast horses saddled—four of 'em—for different points of London. To set off when all's over with the news whether you've blabbed or not.'

Thurtell flung himself back with a laugh. 'Poor wretches! Don't they know Jack Thurtell better than that? They're judging me by themselves, I suppose.' Hunt winced.

'It seems there's a lot of 'em,' the warder went on, 'shaking in their shoes. Because of what you know.'

'Aha! Well, what I know will go down with me in silence. I never blabbed in my life. Not for money and not to save my own neck. Mum has been my word with all pals. It's to be at twelve o'clock noon isn't it?'

'Yes. The chaplain will be with you at nine. Or as early as you request him.'

'He's a good fellow. Here—Hunt—take this book he left with me and read it. There's useful things in it if you give your mind to 'em. And now I'm going to read a little in this one. I've talked enough.'

.   .   .   .   .

At seven o'clock the cell was entered by the sheriff, the governor, the governor's son, and the chaplain. They found Thurtell lying dressed on the bed, in a doze; and Hunt asleep in a chair by the fire. The governor tapped Thurtell on the shoulder. He started up. 'Here's a go! Where am I? Where's the——' Then he saw the governor, and the chaplain, and Hunt, and said, 'Oh. Ah, yes. Well, I'm ready.'

'I'm glad to see you have had some repose,' the chaplain said.

'Yes. I have slept, I think, since two o'clock, and I feel very well. Some odd dreams, but nothing about *this*.'

'You feel composed?'

'Quite composed—in mind and body. I would like to wash.'

'The things shall be brought,' said the governor. 'Will you take a little breakfast?'

'Some tea.'

Water and washing things were brought, and he plunged his head into the basin, and threw the water about his face. The officials standing about watched him and looked at each other in satisfaction at his calm and collected manner, and his urbane behaviour to them. It did not 'go' with all the stories they had heard of the ferocious

Jack Thurtell. They tried to put themselves into his place, and to imagine how they would conduct themselves on such a morning. The result of their imaginings was to give them a respect for this man.

When tea was brought he drank thirstily. When he was drinking his fourth cup the chaplain asked: 'Tell, me Thurtell, is there any last thing we can do for you? Any message you wish sent?'

'Yes; I would be gratefully obliged if you would write to my father, and tell him I made a brave end and that I accept the justice of that end, and die in charity with all mankind. And there is one thing that one of these gentlemen might do for me.'

The sheriff, the governor, and his son came forward. 'Anything you wish, Thurtell, shall be done, so far as the law allows.'

'I would like to know how the great fight went yesterday.'

The men looked at each other again, and seeing Thurtell smiling, they too smiled. 'I have no information,' the governor said, 'but I will have enquiries made outside.' He sent one of the warders on the errand. 'There is nothing else you wish?'

'Nothing. Save that I hope the man will do it quickly and has given me sufficient drop.'

'You may be assured of that. There will be no delay and he has been instructed on the point you mention.' The warder who had been sent away came back breathless. 'Well?'

'The news is that it was a hard battle. It lasted two hours and over, and Tom Spring was badly battered. But he won.'

'That is good news,' Thurtell said, rattling his chains. 'God bless old Tom. I knew him well in other days.'

The governor made a signal to the chaplain, and the chaplain came forward. 'Sir, will you compose yourself with me for half an hour—in preparation for receiving the Sacrament?'

'I will, Sir.'

The chaplain turned to the officials. 'Then let everybody go. Let me be alone with Hunt and Thurtell.'

Thurtell stepped forward and shook rattling hands

with each man present, including the warders. 'God bless you all. Governor—you have been most kind and considerate. You are a good man. You have been a friend to an unworthy man. And these two companions—they have been most sympathetic, and done a dreadful duty with all decency. Joe—may God Almighty look to you. Bless you, bless you. Governor, I have nothing of value to give you, or your son, but he too has been most kind, so perhaps he will accept the only thing I have. This snuff-box. It was given to me by a better man than myself—Mr. Pierce Egan. Pray take it, young man, and God bless you. Chaplain—what I have to say to you may be said in the chapel. May you all be happy. And so, farewell!'

They filed out of the cell and he and Hunt were alone with the chaplain.

.   .   .   .   .

Noon of January 9, 1824. A cold, raw morning, even at its middle, but the space in front of Hertford Gaol was a jam of people. Some of them had been there since midnight, feasting and drinking. The taverns had been open all night, and music and song had filled the dark hours. Since the dawn there had been many quarrels and fights among those who came early and were pushed from their front places by those who came late. When the light came the music and song were dropped: they had a scaffold to look at. Through the night hawkers had done good trade with cakes, sweetmeats, and Last Dying Confessions; and ballad-singers had done well with the Mournful Ballad of Mr. Weare. But with the light, all eyes went to the more mournful—and more thrilling—carpentry in front of the gaol.

By half-past eleven the general feeling in the crowd was that they were being kept waiting. They had affairs to attend, and wanted to get home. But they couldn't get home until this extra-special event had been disposed of. They had paid no money for being present at the event, but they behaved as though they had, and as though the Mayor of Hertford owed them something in the way of a preliminary to the twelve o'clock event.

When the hands of the public clock stood at five minutes before the hour, they became more restless and far more noisy than a theatre audience when the curtain is down fifteen minutes after the advertised time for rising. They shouted. They whistled. They hooted. 'Bring 'im out! Bring 'im out!' They moved and pushed each other, so that the square seemed to be boiling.

But when, at the first stroke of the clock's bell for noon, the doors behind the scaffold opened—then, by some blessed human instinct, the whole square was a pool of silence. Drunk and sober, coarse and gentle, brutal and educated—all were stung to stillness and silence. Hats came off and heads went down. Scarcely any in that crowd knew why they behaved like that; or why they had behaved as they did during the night. The Event was greater than any of them, and greater than their mass.

As John Thurtell stepped out into the light he faced an audience of quiet, almost reverent, figures. He looked down at that rigid mass, and none could have said which of that mass of hatless, bowed men and women were full of liquor or which were sober. They were a mass, gathered for an Event, and the little portion of decency in the vilest of that mass had met all the other portions of decency in full power, and had taken control of the spirit of the mass.

John Thurtell, looking his last on this world, looked on that mass. They might have been gathered for the passing of a noble martyr; but few of the religious martyrs had such a devout and silent company for their passing.

He shook hands with Ruthven, and with the sheriff, and the hangman. Then he took the position he was asked to take. He looked round the crowd from side to side. Down in the front he saw Pierce Egan, who, he knew, was there as a reporter only. He bowed, and Egan gravely acknowledged the bow. Here and there he recognised some of the 'flash coves' of Covent Garden. And another face he recognised, but could not place. Somewhere in the middle of the crowd, standing out from it, was a notably tall young man; a young man whose face he somehow connected with Norwich. He felt that he knew this young man, but he could not place him. He had seen him many times in the past. He was sure of that. But he could not remember who or what this young man was.

As the hangman put the cap over his face, and took three swift steps to another part of the platform, he found himself thinking, not of what was to happen in the next three seconds, but of the name of this young man.

It gave him a fleeting satisfaction that in the second before the floor fell he was able to fix the young man's name as Borrow.